CERTAIN REDEMPTION

CERTAIN REDEMPTION

*The Assurance of God's Perfect Plan For
All Truly Surrendered Christians*

RANDY ADAMS

ReadersMagnet, LLC

CONTENTS

Other books by Randy Adams

The Joy of Assurance (2021)
Just Jesus (2022)
Complacency and Compromise (2023)

Visit www.pastorrandyadams.com for
more information

All of the above books are available on
Amazon

DEDICATION SCRIPTURES:

"In Him we have redemption through His blood, the forgiveness of sins, according to the riches of His grace…"
Ephesians 1:7

"…looking for the blessed hope and glorious appearing of our great God and Savior Jesus Christ, who gave Himself for us, that He might redeem us from every lawless deed and purify for Himself His own special people, zealous for good works."
Titus 2:13-14

All scriptures contained in this book are quoted from the New King James Bible (NKJV)

INTRODUCTION

There are between 9,000 and 10,000 pawnshops in the United States, employing over 70,000 people.[1] Pawnshops have been in existence in one form or another for thousands of years, providing people with a quick and easy way to get small loans of cash by pawning items of market value. Many of the customers are people who have experienced some degree of financial difficulty. Unexpected medical expenses, job loss, or just a way of getting from paycheck to paycheck are some of the reasons for pawning valuable items.

When an item is pawned, the customer receives along with the loaned money what is known as a pawn ticket. That ticket contains the name of the item pawned, the amount of the loan, and the last day that the item can be *redeemed* before it becomes the property of the pawnshop owner, who can then sell the item. The presentation of the pawn ticket is usually required to *redeem* the item. Approximately 60% of items pawned in America are *redeemed* and 40% are not.[2] From the beginning of the transaction the *redemption* of the item is never *certain* or guaranteed if and until the owner of the item returns to *redeem* it.

We as humans are often fickle and forgetful. The day of *redemption* may go by and it will be too late to *redeem* it. The pawn ticket becomes of no value, and the item may be forever lost to the owner. *Redemption* in that case would never take place.

God, on the other hand, is not fickle or forgetful. Unlike a pawnbroker whose promise of *redemption* of a pawned item is conditional, God's promise of *redemption* for those who trust and follow Him is unconditional and absolutely *certain*. His promise is not limited by time or human effort to bring it to pass. For all those who surrender their lives to Jesus based on the completed work of Christ on the cross, *redemption* is *certain*. The hour and the day are yet to be determined, but the promise of God is unchanging. Once in Christ. we belong to Him, and He will not forget His promise to come and *redeem* us in the right moment. God will not *redeem* only 60% of His own. He will *redeem* 100%. Just as the name of the item pawned is contained on a pawn ticket, so all those whose names are written in the Lamb's Book of Life will be those *redeemed* on that day.

When we enter a pawnshop there may be many items for sale that were never *redeemed*. The owner never came back to *redeem* them. We may regard some of the items as *unredeemable* and wonder why anyone would ever have taken them to a pawnshop since they look *corrupted* and beyond *redemption*. Other items for sale may cause us to wonder why someone would have pawned them because they are obviously of great value, such as jewelry or electronic devices. The point is that in either case the owner did not *redeem* them regardless of their face value. In both these cases, on closer inspection, there was probably something faulty or defective, whether the item looked good on the surface or not.

Not everyone will be *redeemed* by Jesus on the day when He comes back as our *Redeemer*. All of humanity has already been *corrupted* by sin and is *unredeemable* from birth. No matter what our face value is on the day that each of us faces the Lord, whether we look beautiful or beyond repair, there is only one way to guarantee our *certain redemption*. Only by surrendering our lives to Jesus and following Him wholeheartedly can we be *assured* of our *redemption* and our names being written in the Lamb's Book of Life.

Job said in Job 19:25, "I know that my Redeemer lives, and He shall stand at last on the earth." Jesus is alive today and is our *Redeemer*. Is your spiritual pawn ticket ready for *redemption* today? Is your name written in the Lamb's Book of Life? Make it *certain* by surrendering your life to Jesus today.

PROLOGUE

We live in a narcissistic society where what true Christianity is supposed to look like is not being modeled well in the modern-day church. To serve Christ faithfully in such a culture requires daily self-examination. Jesus clearly defined what true Christianity is. He said, "Deny yourself, pick up your cross, and follow Me." It begins with self-denial. It is lived out in obedience to the Holy Spirit which indwells every true believer. The apostle Paul reinforced that definition in Galatians 2:20, "I have been crucified with Christ. It is no longer I who live, but Christ who lives in me; and the life I now live in the flesh I live by faith in the Son of God who loved me and gave Himself up for me."

This book is not written to cause any truly surrendered Christian to doubt his or her salvation. In that sense it is a once-saved, always-saved writing. But true salvation *must* begin with surrender. If Christ is truly on the throne of your heart, then this work is written as an assurance of God's *redemptive* plan. Jesus said in John 10:28, "And I give them eternal life, and they shall never perish, neither shall anyone snatch them out of My hand." He also said in John 5:24,

"Most assuredly, I say to you, he who hears My word and believes in Him who sent Me has everlasting life, and shall not come into condemnation, but has passed from death into life."

However, if you are a half-hearted or Sunday morning only Christian, then this work is written to remind you that the *redemption* brought about at an enormous cost on the cross was not accomplished just to free you from hell. If all you want is fire insurance then you cannot call Him "Lord"! Yes, He is your Savior but you must also be willing to *surrender* all and follow Him wholeheartedly as your Lord! Jesus said that on the day of judgment many will say to Him, "I did this for You or I did that in Your name" and He will say to them, "I never knew you." Just give up and follow Him today. He loves you so much and will use you to do great things in His Name if you do. Once in Christ we are to daily desire doing what will bring Him glory! Titus 2:13-14 says, "looking for the blessed hope and glorious appearing of our great God and Savior Jesus Christ, who gave Himself for us, that He might *redeem* us from every lawless deed and purify for Himself His own special people, zealous for good works." Are we eagerly asking every day for divine appointments to do what God has prepared in advance for us to do? God does not expect perfection. We as believers are all still sinners saved by grace alone. We are not already perfect in the sense of sinlessness, but we are *positionally* perfect through Christ's sacrifice if we are truly surrendered. However, everyday we must, as sinners saved by grace, apply the blood of Jesus to our lives and choose obedience over rebellion.

If you are an unbeliever, this book is written as an eye-opener to the inevitability of *redemption* for truly surrendered Christians, regardless of what the unbelieving world may say about it. God would remind you that *certain redemption* is not a myth or a Jewish fairy tale as some in the world would call it. When Jesus said those three final words from the cross, "It is finished!" and bowed His head, it opened the door for the *certain redemption* of all those who would believe and follow Him. The reconciliation of a holy God to sinful man was completed that day for all truly surrendered believers. Jesus became the substitute Lamb of God in that moment to pay for all the sins of all mankind for all time for those who would believe and follow Him. Jesus will come back to *redeem* His church no matter what end times scoffers may pronounce.

The return of the Lord Jesus Christ to the earth to *redeem* His people is foretold repeatedly in the Bible. The *certainty* of it is backed up both historically by events and culturally by ingrained behaviors and traditions.

The unfolding of God's great plan of *redemption* of mankind from sin and death has never been hidden from view. History constantly confirms it. Ingrained customs and practices within people groups worldwide reveal it. Even geography, as we shall see, points to and displays a pattern of deliverance and salvation formed in the heart of God in ages past. The formation of the world and humanity itself, as well as all the events and circumstances orchestrated by God over the last 6,000 years scream the love of God and His plan of salvation to a lost world.

The *certain redemption* of God's people will happen because God says it will. Millions of people will not be a part of that *redemption* because of their refusal to believe and accept the truth of how much Jesus loves them and what He has accomplished for them on the cross. For true followers of Christ, however, *redemption* will take place. Nothing can stop it. No human authority or power, no skeptic, no government, no lie, no deception, and no unbelief can prevent it. If you are an unbeliever in *certain redemption*, start believing in it by surrendering to Christ and you will then become a part of it.

CHAPTER 1

God Is Not Hidden

God, who created the world and everything in it, is not hidden. He is constantly trying to reveal Himself to us. A common cry in the unbelieving world today is, "Where is God? If He is real, why doesn't He make Himself known?" What is not understood is God's unrelenting pursuit of the heart and soul of every human being. It is the carnal mind of sinful mankind, full of pride and self-righteousness, that refuses to realize that God is *shouting* to all of us who He is. Jeremiah 9:23-24 says," 'Let not wise man glory in his wisdom, let not mighty man glory in his might, nor let the rich man glory in his riches; but let him who glories glory in this, that He understands and knows Me, that I am the Lord, exercising lovingkindness, judgment, and righteousness in the earth. For in these I delight,' says the Lord." Jesus delights in our finding Him. This is why the Bible says the angels celebrate in heaven over one sinner who repents.

Knowing God must be a two-way street. He will not force Himself on anyone; He has chosen to give us free will.

We must seek Him to find Him. Deuteronomy 4:29-31 says, "But from there you will seek the Lord your God, and you will find Him if you seek Him with all your heart and all your soul. When you are in distress, and all these things come upon you in the latter days, when you turn to the Lord your God and obey His voice (for the Lord your God is a merciful God), He will not forsake you or destroy you, nor forget the covenant of your fathers which He swore to them." God knows that having an intimate relationship with Him is what is by far the best thing for us. He is constantly pursuing us and trying to reveal Himself to us. He pursued me for 32 years before I yielded myself into His hands.

God has revealed Himself most intimately in the person of Jesus Christ. Jesus came to earth as God in human flesh. What could be more intimate than that? God became one of us at a set time, to teach us, to guide and direct us, to endure suffering which we deserved, and, most of all, to pay the price for our sins through His death on the cross. God desires intimacy with His people. Everything He did for us was done out of His great love for us. What He did as God in a human body is written down for us in the Bible.

In addition to this, God has created a way for even greater intimacy with us today by sending the Holy Spirit to live inside us once we accept and believe in what He accomplished on the cross. Once we believe that He conquered sin on our behalf and conquered death by rising from the dead on the third day, we can then receive the gift of eternal life. As we willingly put our lives in His hands by surrendering and following Him as our Lord as well as our Savior, He comes to us in the most intimate way by the power of the Holy Spirit.

God has revealed Himself to us intimately. To experience His nearness first takes an acknowledgment that we are sinners in need of a Savior. Romans 6:23 says, "For the wages of sin is death, but the gift of God is eternal life in Christ Jesus our Lord." Romans 10:9-10 says, "that if you confess with your mouth the Lord Jesus and believe in your heart that God has raised Him from the dead, you will be saved. For with the heart one believes unto righteousness, and with the mouth confession is made unto salvation." Righteousness by faith is not unreachable and far off, but as near as your heart and your mouth.

Once we are saved it then takes a willingness to put our lives entirely in God's control to experience the fullness of intimacy with Him. That involves not just words but also actions. Deuteronomy 30:14 says, "But the word is very near you, in your mouth and in your heart, that you may do it." Our faith is evidenced by our actions as well as our words. Doing, as well as simply knowing, is vital in practicing our faith.

God has given us both His Word and His Spirit to overcome the temptation to sin. Psalm 119:11 says, "Your word I have hidden in my heart, that I might not sin against You." We must be willing to let go of our carnal mind and worldly thinking and allow His Word by the power of the Holy Spirit to mold us into the image of Christ. Romans 8:6 says, "For to be carnally minded is death, but to be spiritually minded is life and peace." Once Jesus is in control of our lives, we can experience all the joys that intimacy with Him provides.

God does not just want us to know *about* Him. He wants us to know Him *personally*. Think about marriage. Before a couple comes together, at one point they just knew *about* each other. Then they got to know one another *personally*, and finally once married they got to know each other *intimately*. The Bible says they are to become *one* with each other. The same is true with God. He wants to become *one* with each of us by living inside us. And, above all, His motive for revealing Himself to us is love. The Bible says God *is* love. When God truly lives inside us, that love becomes known to those around us as God gives us words to speak and actions to take. Love is God's motive seen throughout the Bible in bringing about our redemption from sin and death, neither of which God ever intended. Love was God's motive in sending Jesus to die on the cross on our behalf. Romans 5:8 says, "But God demonstrates His own love toward us, in that while we were still sinners, Christ died for us."

Love is also God's motive in seeking an intimate relationship with you today. Acts 17:27 says, "so that they should seek the Lord, in the hope that they might grope for Him and find Him, though He is *not far* from each one of us."

CHAPTER 2

The Bible: The Word of God

When I was a kid there was a big Bible in a bookcase at my grandmother's house. My grandparents lived in a small town in the state of Washington where it would get very cold in the winter. I would sit behind an oil heater to stay warm, and I would reach over and pull the Bible out and read stories from Genesis and Exodus. I would sometimes reach over and pet my Aunt Agnes's dog Tiny while I read. Tiny also liked to stay warm behind the oil heater. Sometimes I would even fall asleep sitting there with this big Bible in my lap. Often my aunt would be playing a Tennessee Ernie Ford record on which his crooning voice could be heard singing great old hymns such as "The Old Rugged Cross" and "How Great Thou Art". I remember it as a warm and cozy experience.

One day I decided to venture past the book of Exodus. As I started reading the Book of Leviticus, I did not understand it. In the still unredeemed mind of a nine-year-old boy it seemed boring. I looked ahead at Numbers and Deuteronomy briefly. Same stuff! Sadly, I never picked up that Bible ever again. I never read the New Testament, even though the hymns I was hearing sung were about Jesus and the cross. Instead, unfortunately, I started reading secular books in that same bookcase, such as mystery novels.

I had grown up going with my parents to the Methodist church only on Christmas and Easter since those were the only times during the year that they attended. The church did not emphasize the need for salvation from sin. I had little exposure to the things of God and no interest in learning more about Christ. As a child I considered going to church a drudgery.

As a teenager my parents encouraged me to attend youth events in the basement of the church. In one these events, a group of boys made fun of me, slammed me against the wall, and called me names. I was traumatized and became turned off on church and religion in general. As a matter of fact, as a junior in high school I gave an oral report about the need to discard the Bible as an antiquated book with no contemporary relevance.

It wasn't until years later when I was 25 years old and living with my other grandmother that I finally opened a Bible and read from the four gospels. This grandma watched Billy Graham crusades on television. In one of his sermons Billy spoke about the Pharisees confronting Jesus and claiming Abraham to be their father. Jesus responded to them, "Before Abraham was, I am!" That phrase sparked my curiosity. I remember going to my room, getting out a Bible, and reading those red-letter words. A light went on in my brain in that moment, and I realized for the first time that Jesus was saying that He is God! Unfortunately, I did not act on that knowledge any further for years.

It wasn't until I moved to California and met my future wife Rosalie that I was exposed to the need to completely surrender my life to Jesus. Rosalie had been saved at that time for over ten years. She told me if I wanted to continue dating her I had to go to church. On February 2, 1982, when I was 32 years old, I finally gave my life to Christ. I remember going to church the next Sunday, and as the pastor preached from the book of Nehemiah, the words seemed to leap out at me. The Holy Spirit was now resident in my life and was enlightening the Word of God in my mind and my heart.

The Bible is God's number one way of revealing Himself to humanity. It is God's love letter to a lost and dying world. Every part of the Bible fits together with every other part in perfection. It has been proved historically. It has been proved archeologically. It has survived the ages intact and flawless. It is completely unlike any other written document in human history, and is also a history of humanity up through the end of the first century A.D. Every part of the Bible points to Jesus as the Savior of the world. He is the only way to get to heaven when we die. John 14:6 might very well be the most important verse in the Bible, where Jesus said, "I am the way, the truth, and the life. No man comes to the Father except through Me." Jesus is God revealed to mankind as both man and God. He truly is "Immanuel, God with us". Jesus is alive today because He conquered death by rising from the grave. He is the *living* Word of God. When you see Jesus, you see God! John 1:18 says, "No one has seen God at any time.

The only begotten Son, who is in the bosom of the Father, He has declared Him." God became visible to human eyes in the person of Jesus. It is through seeing the Son that we see God. The Bible is, in effect, Jesus in a book. The Bible reveals the totality of who Jesus is.

The Bible is a complete and reliable source of what God has spoken about Himself through the minds and writings of men. The number of Biblical manuscripts preserved through the ages is far greater than any other ancient writing. There are roughly 6000 preserved manuscripts of the New Testament alone.[3] The closest contender is Homer's Iliad, which has only 600 existing copies.[4] In addition, the Biblical manuscripts are nearly identical to each other, and any minor changes due to translation do not affect the theology. The finding of the Dead Sea scrolls in the 1940's verified the authenticity of the Old Testament manuscripts almost to the letter.

Many archeological finds also support scripture, even in minor detail. The recent uncovering of the pool of Siloam and the pool of Bethesda in Jerusalem is one example. Another is the finding of the anchors off the coast of Malta described in the Book of Acts when Paul was shipwrecked. More findings will be discussed in a later chapter.

40 authors wrote the Bible over a period of 1500 years, yet every part fits prophetically, doctrinally and theologically with every other part. Every book points to Jesus Christ as the author of our *certain redemption*, purchased at the cross.

All scripture is inspired by the Holy Spirit. 2 Timothy 3:16 says, "All Scripture is given by inspiration of God, and is profitable for doctrine, for reproof, for correction, for instruction in righteousness,". Another version says that all Scripture is "God-breathed". Can you imagine the very breath of God providing for us a perfect work, revealing not only who He is, but who we are to become in Him. The revelation and absolute *certainty* of His *redemptive* plan is confirmed over and over in the Bible.

The Word of God and its great value and importance to all believers is confirmed within its own pages, especially in Psalm 119 as well as Psalm 19. In each of these psalms there are multiple nouns which refer to the Word of God and the revelation of who God is. These nouns refer to the Word of God as testimonies, laws, commandments, precepts, judgments, statutes, and ways. Following each of these nouns is found practical emphasis on their value for everyday living. Each noun reveals one of the many different and wonderful ways God wants to speak to us. Psalm 119, with 176 verses, is both the longest chapter in the Bible as well as the exact middle chapter of the Bible. These facts point to the immense importance of not just knowing the Word but living it out daily. The exhortations contained in these two psalms tell every seeker of God how to know Him more. The main way to do that is to seek Him through His Word. The placement of Psalm 119 is a testament to the perfection of the Bible; if anyone picks up a Bible, even by accident, and opens it to the middle, they will find one of the greatest places in Scripture which reveals who God is and how to find Him.

Finally, Psalm 119 was written for the application of God's Word to our lives by faith. For example, verse 11 tells us hiding it in our hearts keeps us from sinning. Verse 105 reveals it as a lamp for our feet and a light for our path. Verse 111 uses the word heritage, indicating its value from generation to generation. In addition, the word *revive* is found eleven times in Psalm 119, more than anywhere else in the Bible. Revival means bringing spiritual vitality back to our lives and our souls. By faith we apply the Word to bring conviction, direction, durability and renewal to our lives.

The word *redeem* is mentioned twice in Psalm 119, once in verse 134 to ask for *redemption* from human oppression and once in verse 154 to ask for *redemption* that leads to revival. Only in the person of Jesus Christ can these two entreaties ultimately be fulfilled. Only through the blood of Jesus can we be spiritually revived, and only through His resurrection can we now truly say, "What can man do to me?"

The Bible not only reveals who God is, it reveals who we are in Him. As we apply His Word by faith we will see the transformation of our own lives. The book I once saw as antiquated and of no value is the only true map of life in a broken world. Hebrews 4:12 says, "For the word of God is living and powerful, and shaper than any two-edged sword, piercing even to the division of soul and spirit, and of joints and marrow, and is a discerner of the thoughts and intents of the heart." The *certain redemption* that is the hope of all true followers of Christ is the treasure that awaits those who walk by faith and allow the Word to pierce us and mold us and transform us into the image of Christ.

CHAPTER 3

The Holy Spirit

In John 14:16-18 Jesus said, "And I will pray the Father, and He will give you another Helper, that He may abide with you forever – the Spirit of truth, whom the world cannot receive, because it neither sees Him nor knows Him; but you know Him, for He dwells with you and will be in you. I will not leave you as orphans; I will come to you." It could not be clearer from this passage that the way God had already revealed Himself to humanity in the person of Jesus Christ would now be kicked up a notch, so to speak, to an even greater level of intimacy for those who believe in God's completed work on the cross. Jesus in His human body could only be in one place at a time. But now the third person of the Trinity, the Holy Spirit, would come to live inside believing persons, providing the most intimate knowledge of and presence of God Himself. The role of God performing miracles in the person of Jesus would now be taken over by the Holy Spirit in Jesus name. This would provide to all the known world a greater revelation of the power and authority of God. It would also point to the reality of and certain outcome of God's *redemptive* plan.

Jesus also said in John 14:26, "But the Helper, the Holy Spirit, whom the Father will send in My name, He will teach you all things, and bring to your remembrance all things that I said to you." It is the role of the Holy Spirit to enlighten all that Jesus has said in His Word to us as Christ followers. I can testify in my own walk with Christ that when I was preparing for ministry or writing a book the Holy Spirit would constantly and consistently bring to my mind scriptures, with the intent of using them to accomplish God's purposes. It all began the day after I got saved in Pasadena, California, when, for the first time, the Bible seemed not only to make sense to me, but also to speak directly and personally to my heart. This is the role of the Holy Spirit in the life of every believer. The more we as followers of Jesus expand our knowledge of God's Word, the more material the Holy Spirit has, so to speak, to mold us and make us into the image of Christ. It is our duty as believers to listen to the Spirit as we read the Bible and obey His directives. He will always lead us to situations and circumstances that are for our ultimate good, even though sometimes what is spoken to us to say or to do may seem impossible or even "crazy" to our limited minds and consciousness. Yielding our carnal mind to the mind of the Spirit is not always easy, but it is always ultimately beneficial. Romans 8:28 says, "And now we know that *all* things work together for good to those who love God, to those who are called according to His purpose."

The Holy Spirit, our Helper, helps us overcome the carnal mind for our own good. Romans 8:5-6 says, "For those who live according to the flesh set their minds on the things of the flesh, but those who live according to the Spirit the things of the Spirit. For to be carnally minded is death, but to be spiritually minded is life and peace." We cannot overcome our carnal thoughts by ourselves. We are all born as sinners, and we all have the sin nature. While Jesus paid the full price for our sins on the cross, we still need our Helper to overcome all our fleshly thoughts and tendencies, and to help prevent us from giving in to worldly temptations. That's one big reason why Jesus said in John 16:7, "Nevertheless I tell you the truth. It is to your advantage that I go away; for if I do not go away, the Helper will not come to you; but if I depart, I will send Him to you." Praise God for the day of Pentecost and the giving to us as followers of Christ the Holy Spirit! It is only by the Spirit that we can be made into the image of Jesus. It is only by the Spirit that we can live lives that truly honor and reflect God to a lost and dying world.

The Holy Spirit also consistently and constantly points to and confirms God's great *redemptive* plan. Even in the Old Testament, as the Spirit spoke through the prophets, the overriding emphasis was restoration and *redemption*. Even when it was the Lord's purpose to bring judgment on His people because of their idolatry and rebellion, the end goal of every act of God was ultimately *redemptive*. Again and again among the prophets we see the Spirit speaking impending judgment, but then followed by passages of restoration. Often these scriptures point to periods of restoration of the Israelites in the centuries before Christ was born. For example, Jeremiah 50:34 says this, "Their Redeemer is strong; the Lord of hosts is His name; He will thoroughly plead their case, that He may give rest to the land, and disquiet the inhabitants of Babylon." In contrast sometimes these passages point to the ultimate *Redeemer* Himself, the Lord Jesus Christ. A good example of this is found in Micah 5:2 where the Spirit through the words of the prophet Micah point to the birthplace of Jesus: "But you, Bethlehem Ephrathah, though you are little among thousands of Judah, yet out of you shall come forth to Me the One to be Ruler in Israel, whose goings forth are from of old, from everlasting." Finally, some of these Spirit-led scriptures refer to the *certain redemption* of all followers of Christ in the end times in which we live. One specific scripture points to that time. It describes it as a time when the knowledge of the Lord will be universal and our *certain redemption* will already have taken place: Habakkuk 2:14 says, "For the earth will be filled with the knowledge of the glory of the Lord, as the waters cover the sea."

The *certain redemptive* plan of the Lord is also made apparent by the Holy Spirit throughout the New Testament, not just through the life and words of Jesus Himself in the gospels, but also in the Pauline epistles, and particularly in the book of Hebrews, the author of which is basically unknown. Referring to Christ, the author of Hebrews writes in Hebrews 9:12, "Not with the blood of goats and calves, but with His own blood He entered the Most Holy Place once for all, having obtained *eternal redemption*." The scripture goes on in verse 15, "And for this reason He is the Mediator of the new covenant, by means of death, for the *redemption* of the transgressions under the first covenant, that those who are called may receive the promise of the *eternal inheritance*." In this last scripture the word *redemption* is expanded from its implied meaning under the Law. The old covenant pointed primarily to *physical* redemption from bondages brought about mostly through rebellion and idolatry. The *redemption* from the *penalty of sin* under the old covenant is still a matter of some debate, and certainly was not applied universally to all sin, at least not in that dispensation of time. Hebrews 9:7 indicates that the blood of animal sacrifices was offered by the high priest "for himself and for the people's sins committed *in ignorance*." It did not cover *premeditated* sins or the sinful nature of all people. The old covenant was lacking and did not totally reconcile the people to God.[5] All sacrifices under the Mosaic law were only a foreshadowing of the perfect and final sacrifice of Christ on the cross.

The *redemption* from the penalty of *all* sin, past, present and future for all those who surrender their lives to Jesus occurred when He bowed His head and said "It is finished!" The blood of Jesus shed on the cross made *redemption certain* for all true followers of Christ throughout all the centuries that have gone by since. The *eternal inheritance* is dangling in front of our very eyes, urging us to be steadfast and faithful servants to the very end.

We must realize the *enormity* and *timelessness* of Christ's sacrifice for sins. God exists outside of time. Jesus merely stepped into time and then out again, back into eternity. The work He completed when He died for sin was an eternal and everlasting work, stretching back in time to the creation of the world and forward to the new heaven and the new earth. Therefore, all Old Testament saints were also forgiven based on Christ's sacrifice, which still lay in the future during the dispensation of time in which they lived. Otherwise, they would not be listed in the hall of faith in Hebrews 11 or make appearances, such as Moses and Elijah on the Mount of Transfiguration. The sins of all those listed in the hall of faith are never mentioned by the writer of Hebrews. By the time Hebrews was written the work of Christ in forgiving sins had been completed. The sins of the patriarchs, as well as our sins, are not remembered by God once we surrender to Jesus. Their sins, our sins, and all sins of all people of all time, were forgiven through the precious blood of Jesus. However, it must be believed in and applied to our lives in the form of surrender to Jesus and His purposes for us to participate in *certain redemption*. The curse which came upon mankind in the Garden of Eden was *eternally reversed* by Jesus on the cross! It simply takes total surrender of our lives into the hands of the One who loves us so much! How can we possibly take for granted the fact that the Bible says when God sees us *in Christ* that God sees us with His righteousness and with our sins blotted out forever? A true understanding of the enormity of what Jesus has done for us should drive us to our knees and prostrate ourselves before Him in worship and adoration!

The incredible depth of the love of God is comprehended in greater measure as we listen to and *obey* the Holy Spirit.

Obedience always leads to blessing. I said this hundreds of times from the pulpit as a pastor. Perhaps the greatest blessing of obedience is gaining a deeper understanding of how great the love of God is. The Lord Jesus chastens the church in Ephesus in the Book of Revelation for having lost their first love. A loveless church is where the Holy Spirit does not feel welcome or is quenched by the presence of sin. A loveless church is where religion has replaced a relationship with God. When the will of man surpasses the will of God, experiencing the love of God in all its fullness is all but snuffed out. In his letters it is obvious that the apostle Paul had a burden for churches he had been led by the Lord to establish. Paul included prayers in these letters, all of which are there to be a model for us in praying for our churches. Perhaps Paul's most poignant prayer is the one he prays for the loveless church in Ephesus. Ephesians 3:14-21 reveals the heart of Paul in asking the Lord to show the Ephesian church how once again how amazing is the love of God for them. I include here a portion of that prayer. Ephesians 3:17-19 says, "that Christ may dwell in your hearts through faith; that you, being rooted and grounded in love, may be able to comprehend with all the saints what is the width and length and depth and height – to know the love of Christ which passes knowledge; that you may be filled with all the fullness of God." We can pray that same prayer for our churches so that the Holy Spirit can have free reign in our midst. The curse of sin has been broken! The cross is empty and the greatest act of love in the history of the world has been accomplished! All Jesus asks is that we follow Him obediently! Obedience in this life leads to the blessing of living an abundant life. Obedience ultimately leads to hearing the words, "Well done, good and faithful servant", when we get to heaven. Finally, obedience leads to the excitement of following where the Holy Spirit leads us daily in this life.

Justification by faith alone is a theme woven throughout the Bible, however that faith must be genuine and include a willingness to forsake all and follow Christ. This is a hard saying for half-hearted or lukewarm Christians. I think Peter made it most clear in his last letter to the church which was already being compromised and full of doubters and skeptics. 2 Peter 1:10 says, "Therefore, brethren, be even more diligent to make your call and election sure, for if you do these things you will never stumble;". The *things* that Peter is referring to in this verse are found in verses 5 to 7 of the same chapter. These *things* are added to faith to give us a measuring rod to make sure that our faith is truly genuine, and that we are therefore truly saved. The seven *things* Peter refers to are virtue, knowledge, self-control, perseverance, godliness, brotherly kindness and love. These seven characteristics of a truly redeemed person, along with nine fruit of the Spirit in Galatians 5:22, provide a daily formula for every follower of Christ for self-examination. Peter is not speaking here about losing our salvation; he is merely reminding us that if we fall short in any of these areas of our lives, we need to repent and then keep going. He reminds us in 2 Peter 1:9, "For he who lacks these *things* is shortsighted, even to blindness, and has forgotten that He was cleansed from his old sins."

As believers we can so easily start to take for granted the *enormity* of what Jesus did on the cross and start to drift away little by little. The writer of Hebrews warns us against this in Hebrews 2:1, "Therefore we must give the more earnest heed to the things we have heard lest we *drift* away." This was what Peter was warning against in his last letter before being martyred. This was Peter's great concern as well as the infiltration of false teachers and prophets into the church.

It is the role of the Holy Spirit to bring us to that point of self-examination as we use those benchmarks provided in 2 Peter 1:5-7 and Galatians 5:22. The Helper will bring conviction to us as we read the Word. Conviction is a good thing, and it causes us to compare our walk to the perfect walk of Jesus. There are two scriptures in Proverbs 3:11-12 which are repeated in Hebrews 12:5-6 that refer to the concept of *chastening*. To *chasten* means to make someone understand that they have failed or done something wrong and encourage them to improve.[6] Biblically it implies correction or discipline with the goal of refining our words and behavior to be more like Christ. In a nutshell, it is *spiritual training*. When we are in physical training, we often use a *trainer*. One of the functions of the Holy Spirit is to be our *spiritual trainer*. When we mess up as Christians it is important that we allow the Holy Spirit to train us. He will help us get back on course if we have drifted or become a straying sheep. God sends His Spirit to help us through problems and troubles, often of our own making because of giving in to temptation. Jesus sends the Spirit to bring us back into the fold like the shepherd leaving the 99 to get the one. Sometimes our sin leads to suffering, and the Lord may allow the consequences of sin as a form of *chastening*. Whether our unpleasant circumstances were brought about by our own drifting, or only because we live in a corrupted world, the Holy Spirit is there to remind us that we have not yet suffered as much as Jesus suffered on our behalf. Hebrews 12: 4 says, "You have not yet resisted to bloodshed, striving against sin." Jesus resisted the temptation to not "drink the cup" of suffering which lay ahead of Him in the Garden of Gethsemane, so much so that "His sweat became like great drops of *blood* falling down to the ground." Our Helper is there to both show us the way out when we are tempted, as well as to *chasten* us when we give in to temptation and find ourselves in a sinful mess. It is up to us to let Him do His job.

Once the Holy Spirt has worked in our lives to bring us to that point of total surrender, and having made our call and election sure as we daily measure our walk with Christ by the fruit of our labors, we can then truly be assured of our justification in the sight of God and His plan for our *certain redemption*. There are a number of places in the Bible where the Holy Spirit using the minds and hearts of men has written scriptures which point to and affirm justification by faith and faith alone. Some of these scriptures are more well-known than others in this regard. The following two scriptures, one in the Old Testament and one in the New Testament, support this doctrine in ways that should bring grateful tears to our eyes as followers of Jesus.

The first scripture is Isaiah 44:22, "For I have blotted out, like a thick cloud, your transgressions, and like a cloud, your sins. Return to Me, for I have redeemed you." As mentioned earlier, the blood of Christ paid the price in full for all sins from the beginning of time to the end of it for all true believers, including the Old Testament patriarchs and all those who truly followed God. To blot out means to erase, as if the sin had never been committed. All the Old Testament saints were *redeemed* or bought back in the pre-incarnation dispensation of time by the blood of Christ because God exists outside of time and sees the end from the beginning. Notice how this scripture is written in the past tense, meaning that *both* justification and redemption have already occurred. The best example of this is the faith of Abraham who simply believed what God said when He told him that his descendants would be as many as the stars in the sky. Genesis 15:6 says, "And he believed in the Lord, and He accounted it to him for righteousness." Regardless that after this Abraham would sin more than once by lying about Sarah being his sister and by later sleeping with Hagar, he was already justified or made righteous in the sight of God simply by believing what He said and following Him as a result. In Isaiah 44:22 we not only find the concept of justification by faith but also the concept of ongoing sanctification. The three words, "Return to Me", spoken through the prophet Isaiah, speak to us today as a daily mandate. Returning to God is a daily process for the believer that will last until he or she takes his or her last breath. Sanctification is being molded little by little into the image of Christ, who is God. At one point I was not familiar with Isaiah 44:22 but the Lord brought it to me in a dream which I shall never forget.

In my dream Jesus was checking boxes in fulfillment of prophetic scripture. At the end of my dream He said, "I have also fulfilled Isaiah 44:22". I had to run and get my Bible and look up this scripture. When I read it I wept. God's grace and mercy are immeasurable and without limit.

The second scripture supporting the doctrine of justification by faith is found in Hebrews 10:14, "For by one offering He has perfected forever those who are being sanctified." It is very important to understand what the word "perfected" means in this context. It does not mean already perfect in the sense of sinlessness but rather *positionally* perfect through Christ's sacrifice on the cross. The words "made righteous" or "justified" could be substituted here without changing the meaning significantly. The other key word is "being" as it relates to sanctification. This scripture clearly indicates that followers of Christ as all still "works in progress" in this life, in the process of *being* sanctified and made into the image of Christ. 2 Corinthians 5:21 reminds us why we are now seen as righteous, "For He made Him who knew no sin to *be* sin for us, that we might become the righteousness of God in Him." The divine exchange in which Jesus takes all our sin and gives us all of His righteousness should give rise to awe at the amazing love of God. The incredible depth of His love should motivate us to not take for granted what God has done but rather be diligent to trust and obey Him day by day. The point here is that God wants us to live in absolute assurance of who we are positionally in Jesus, but at the same time be careful to examine ourselves daily in terms of fruitfulness to make sure we are still walking in the light as He sheds the light. It is another function of the Holy Spirit to warn us when we are getting off into the shadows and becoming too worldly.

In the original King James version of the Bible, the Holy Spirit is also referred to as our Comforter. Strength and reassurance for believers in need is the role of the Holy Spirit as Comforter.[7] This can be as simple as being the One who reminds us of the *certain redemption* that lies ahead for us, as long as we keep on keeping on as the apostle Paul exhorts us to do, or as complex as bringing that "peace that passes all understanding" to bear when grief or loss takes place. 2 Corinthians 1:3-4 says, "Blessed be the God and Father of our Lord Jesus Christ, the Father of mercies and God of all *comfort*, who *comforts* us in all our tribulation, that we may be able to comfort those who are in any trouble, with the *comfort* with which we ourselves are *comforted* by God." God always takes trials and tries to turn them into testimonies. We must listen to and obey the Holy Spirit, not only receiving the *comfort* of the *Holy Spirit during the trial, but also passing along the true story of that comfort* to those who may be experiencing the same type of problem or difficulty, even months or years later.

Another function of the Holy Spirit is the effectuation of the gifts of the spirit found in Romans 12 and 1 Corinthians 12. Once we surrender to Christ and His presence indwells us, there are spiritual gifts available for us which are to be used for the edification of the body of Christ and the winning of the lost. Some of these gifts are simply the use of natural talents we already possess, while others are implemented and used miraculously. The issue of the enactment of these gifts by the Holy Spirit has brought about much division in the modern-day church, including the difference between evangelical and pentecostal doctrine as to the role of the Holy Spirit in this area. Volumes could be written regarding the interpretation of this function of the Holy Spirit which are beyond the scope of this book. Suffice it to say at this point that the miracles which *still do take place* as effectuated by the Holy Spirit is one of the living proofs that God is not hidden. It is one method God uses to reveal Himself today.

Throughout scripture the Holy Spirit points to the fact that Jesus died to provide *redemption* to "buy back" those who have put their faith in Him. Jesus died to pay the price required to ransom sinners. If someone is kidnapped and a ransom is then paid, the person taken hostage is then set free. 1 Peter 1:18-20 in the New Living Translation emphasizes this analogy, "For you know that God paid a ransom to save you from the empty life you inherited from your ancestors. And it was not paid with mere gold or silver, which lose their value. It was [paid with] the precious blood of Christ, the sinless, spotless Lamb of God. God chose Him as your ransom long before the world began". We are set free from being hostages to the sin nature when Jesus "buys us back". Once we are bought and are His, we can then live in assurance of His coming back to take us to be with Him where He is at. As surrendered believers we are already citizens of heaven, and we can look forward to our *certain redemption* when Jesus appears in the eastern sky. Romans 3:23-26 says, "for all have sinned and fall short of the glory of God, being justified freely by His grace through the *redemption* that is in Christ Jesus, whom God set forth as a propitiation by His blood, through faith, to demonstrate His righteousness, because in His forbearance God had passed over the sins that were previously committed, to demonstrate at the present time His righteousness, that He might be just and the *justifier of the one who has faith in Jesus."*

CHAPTER 4

Answered Prayer

There is nothing more affirming of the presence of God than answered prayer. When we clearly realize that situations and circumstances have changed because of the hand of God, whether it be through provision, protection, healing or clear guidance, it greatly increases our faith. James 5:16 concludes, "The effective, fervent prayer of a righteous man avails much." Since we as followers of Jesus have the righteousness of Christ upon us, we can believe that yes, indeed, our prayers will avail much as long as we seek Him and pray according to His will.

There are many biblical examples of answered prayer. James goes on in chapter 5 by giving the example of Elijah. James 5:17-18 says, "Elijah was a man with a nature like ours, and he prayed earnestly that it would not rain; and it did not rain on the land for three years and six months. And he prayed again, and the heaven gave rain, and the earth produced its fruit." James refers to Elijah as a man with a nature like ours, meaning we should not put him on a pedestal because he was a mighty prophet and taken up into heaven in a whirlwind. Peter made that mistake at the Mount of Transfiguration when he put Elijah and Moses on the same level as Jesus by asking for three equal tabernacles; the result was the voice of the Father from heaven affirming that Jesus was the Messiah, His only Son. In other words, Elijah was human just like any of us who are saved by the grace and mercy of God. It is important to realize, however, that the prayers of Elijah changed the weather only because it was God's will that it would happen. It is possible for us to pray outside the will of God and become frustrated because we don't see anything happening. This is usually the result of not asking to see things from God's perspective and not our own before we ask. The other issue, of course, is waiting for God's perfect timing and not our own.

Sometimes we wait until we are in trouble before we turn to God in prayer. Often the trouble can be of our own making because of giving in to temptation and sinning. The perfect biblical example of this is Jonah. When he was running away from Ninevah as fast and as far as he could, he thought he could outrun or hide from God. The last thing he wanted to do was pray. It wasn't until God sent a storm on the sea to almost sink the ship that he realized his rebellion was affecting not just his life but the lives of others on the ship. He knew by throwing him overboard they would be delivered. He was ready to face death, but still did not pray. Even the men on the ship prayed for God's help before Jonah was willing to. It wasn't until he was in the belly of the great fish that he finally cried out to God. His prayer of worship and contrition resulted in God giving him another chance by having the fish vomit him onto dry land. The lesson here is to trust and obey God and pray for His help in accomplishing the task He has assigned to you. Even when our feelings go against the idea of obeying and following God, we need to be on our knees asking for Him to go before us and prepare the land and the people ahead of time to receive the message God has given us. This is what divine appointments are all about in the time in which we live. It is always God's will for us to share the gospel as commanded by Jesus in the Great Commission. Even then we must listen to the promptings of the Holy Spirit and obey in His timing and according to His will.

One of the best examples of obedience in response to a divine appointment is found in Acts 8:26-40. Philip the evangelist was told by an angel of the Lord to go down the road from Jerusalem to Gaza. He obeyed and came across an Ethiopian eunuch of great authority reading the prophetic scriptures about Jesus in the book of Isaiah. The Spirit told Philip to go near and overtake the chariot of the eunuch. In verse 30 the scripture says that Philip *ran* to the Ethiopian. He did not hesitate; he did not question why. Philip then, beginning at the scripture in Isaiah, preached Jesus to him. This was not the first time that Philip had responded in obedience to the Spirit. In Acts 8:4 he went to Samaria to preach Christ. Both Samaria and Gaza were places where Gentiles dwelled. The apostles, including even Peter, had not been obedient in going out from Jerusalem in response to the command of Jesus in Acts 1:8 to go "in all Judea and Samaria, and to the end of the earth". God will use a willing vessel. Philip was willing. He was not Philip the apostle but rather one of the elders chosen in Acts 6:5 to serve tables, make sure widows were not neglected, and do other works. He was used by the Lord to evangelize and perform miracles by the Spirit. In Acts 21:8 we find him continuing to evangelize, this time in Caesarea Philippi. We must remember as followers of Christ that listening to and obeying the Spirit is just as important as seeking the Spirit. The Spirit is sought in prayer. The Spirit speaks and prompts in prayer. It is then with arms, legs and mouths that we obey and become the answer to our own prayer. If you ask for divine appointments the Lord will give them to you. In James 4:2 the Bible says you have not because you ask not. It goes on to say in verse 3 that we "ask and do not receive, because you ask amiss, that you may spend it on your pleasures." We must pray for things that God desires to see in our lives. Pray for provision that facilitates ministry. Pray for protection while doing God's will. Pray most of all that He will use you as a vessel and a mouthpiece. Pleasures are fleeting and have no eternal value. Souls saved should be the ultimate goal in our prayer lives.

Another biblical example of answered prayer is found in the life of King Hezekiah in 2 Kings 20:1-7. Isaiah the prophet had told the king that he should set his house in order because he was about to die. Hezekiah then pleaded with the Lord to remember his loyal heart. He wept. Then the Lord spoke again through Isaiah and said to Hezekiah in verses 5-6, "I have heard your prayer, I have seen your tears; surely I will heal you. On the third day you shall go up to the house of the Lord. And I will add to your days fifteen years." The question based on this biblical text becomes, "Can I similarly plead my case before the Lord and ask Him to change what is about to happen?" Isaiah 43:26 says, "Put Me in remembrance; let us contend together; state your case, that you may be acquitted."

In 1985 that is exactly what I did. My father's esophagus ruptured, and the contents of his stomach escaped into the pericardium around his heart. I received a call from my mom in the middle of the night saying that the doctor suggested that she call the family home because my father might not live another day. I caught a flight to Portland, Oregon, from Southern California where my wife Rosalie and I were living. As I was landing in Portland the day was starting to dawn, and I prayed that my father would live until I got to Roseburg which is 186 miles south of Portland. I rented a car and drove three hours and went directly to the hospital. My mom and I met with the doctor who said there was only a 10% chance that my dad would survive. The hospital had sent to the east coast for some special antibiotics to fight the infection around his heart.

I went in to see my dad in ICU, and they had him on a ventilator. He recognized me and grabbed my hands and kissed them with tears running down his cheeks which the nurse had to wipe away. I was moved with great love and compassion for my dad in that moment, especially considering he was not a man who wore his emotions on his sleeve. There was a chapel in the hospital where my mom and brothers and I went to pray.

The doctor finally told us to go home for a few hours, and that he would call us if things worsened. Early the next morning, I went for a walk. Behind my parents' home was a big hill. I hiked up to the top, and from there I could see the roof of the hospital in the far distance. I got down on my knees, and I pleaded my case and the case of my mom and brothers before the Lord. I begged Jesus to heal my dad, or at least to give him more time. I remembered the prayer of King Hezekiah, and how the Lord gave him fifteen more years. So that is what I asked the Lord for. I asked God to give my dad fifteen years additional life.

The next day the antibiotics arrived from the east coast, and they started them on an IV. The doctors told us that surgery was urgent to staple his esophagus shut and insert a tube in his stomach. He said there was less than a 50% chance that my dad would even survive the operation. As the surgery progressed, we all prayed in the chapel. Not only did my father survive, after six weeks he was sent home from the hospital, still unable to eat, and with a feeding tube in his stomach.

Six months later he was scheduled for another surgery to reconnect his esophagus. I flew to Oregon again, and the surgery was successful. For all those six months my father was being prayed for in a Sunday school that I attended at Lake Avenue Congregational Church in Pasadena. A year later my mom and dad moved to Southern California, and my dad went to work with me in my job as an accountant. He and my mom went to church with Rosalie and I. When he walked into the Sunday school, everyone stood and gave

God a standing ovation. I grew closer to my dad during this time than at any other time in my life.

In 2000 my father's health started to decline; he had given up smoking before the incident in 1985, but his lungs began to deteriorate from all the damage it had done. The month in which my dad almost died in 1985 was August. My dad passed away and went to be with Jesus on August 16, 2000, almost fifteen years to the day from when I prayed on that hill looking toward the hospital. God listens to the pleadings of those who seek Him. All during those fifteen years my dad would often say, "each day is a plus". When my mom called me the night my dad died, Rosalie and I came to her. My dad was still sitting in his chair, and his body was still warm. I took his hands and kissed them, just as he had taken my hands and kissed them fifteen years earlier. His healing and subsequent life have become a testimony to the power of prayer, and the fact that God *does* listen to and answer our pleadings. I can't wait to see my dad and mom in heaven.

It is important to remember that God answers prayer in His timing and not our own. Waiting on God is not always easy, especially in a culture that expects everything to happen instantly. I think it was easier for Christians to wait on God before the industrial revolution, and especially before instant telecommunication. Today we can get the answer to anything so quickly. Just google it. But we can't google God. We must always keep in mind that God is *good*. He will always answer prayer in a way that is *best* for us, even when we don't think it is best. Remember that God sees the end from the beginning.

That will help when we struggle with timing. He is both sovereign and He is so *good*.

The power of prayer within the body of Christ cannot be overestimated. God still does miracles of healing, provision and protection today. However, seeing miracles should not be our primary reason for seeking God. Often when Jesus performed a miracle, he would warn the person who received it not to spread word of it, even sometimes warning his disciples as well. An example of that is found in Mark 5:21-43 when Jairus, one of the synagogue rulers, begged Jesus to heal his daughter who was deathly ill. Later, when Jesus raised her from the dead, verse 43 says, "He commanded them strictly that no one should know it…" Jesus did not want to be known primarily as a miracle worker, lest people seek Him for the wrong reasons.[8] Jesus always wants us to seek Him not just for what He can do, but for who He is. His primary mission in coming to earth the first time was not just to do miracles of healing, but to accomplish the greatest miracle of all on the cross. His death on the cross provided freedom for all those who believe and follow Him not just from physical infirmity but from the wages of sin which is death and eternal separation from God.

Jesus wants us to seek Him because we are sinners in need of a Savior. Does He do miracles of healing today? Yes, but only in His timing and for His purposes. He may have a greater purpose than the healing itself. Remember that the apostle Paul prayed three times that the thorn in his flesh be taken away from him, but in 2 Corinthians 12:9, the Lord said to him, "My grace is sufficient for you, for My strength is made perfect in weakness." Often we look only at only the first part of what the Lord said to Paul. His amazing grace and love poured out for us on the cross in the end is really all we need. However, notice how the Lord actually gave Paul the *reason* why He chose not to heal him. The way Paul dealt with the thorn in the flesh would become an example to all those around him. They would see how God was giving him the strength to carry on and complete the work given to him in spite of his infirmity. God can take infirmity and weakness and turn it into a testimony. We need to realize that than the actual healing of our bodies is the salvation of those around us who can see how Jesus guides us through the storms of life. To repeat a simple truth, God is in control. He is sovereign in the affairs of men. He sees the end from the beginning. He will work out circumstances and situations to accomplish His purpose no matter how we feel about it. It is so important for followers of Christ to walk by faith and not by feelings.

That still takes us back, however, to the fact God hears, honors, and answers prayer made in supplication and in His will. For example, in the Book of Acts, the church was gathered in prayer to seek the release of Peter from prison. The word used to describe their prayer in Acts 12:5 is *constant*. 1 Thessalonians 5:17 tells us today as believers to "pray constantly" or "pray without ceasing", which means basically having a lifestyle of prayer and listening to God. When followers of Christ gather with a common purpose in prayer in the will of God, He is pleased. The pursuit of God with one mind and one accord frees the Holy Spirit to move in power. The believers in the Book of Acts were seen as righteous in the sight of God not because of any work they were doing, but rather because of the atoning death of Jesus on their behalf. It is the same for us today. When we are truly surrendered to the Lord, and gather in His name, He is in the midst and invites us by the power of the Holy Spirit to seek His face, know His will and then see it come to pass.

The answer to the prayer of the church in Acts 12 involved God sending an angel to open the prison doors for Peter. It was so miraculous that Peter thought he was dreaming. The reaction of the believers praying for Peter teaches us a lesson as well. We must not doubt the answer to our prayers even when it seems *impossible*, for with God all things are *possible*. In a way the story becomes humorous. They dismissed the young girl Rhoda when she came running and swearing that Peter was at the door. We must remember that more important than *astonishment* at miraculous answers to prayer is gratefulness and giving all glory to God.

Another personal example of answered prayer in my own life occurred in 2009. I was in the parking lot at work when I got a call from my doctor. I had been experiencing some pain in my lower back. He informed me that I had been diagnosed with multiple myeloma, a cancer which forms tumors in the plasma part of blood. These tumors then cling to bones. In my case the tumors were clinging to my pelvis. My wife immediately put me on the prayer line in church. The pain became so debilitating that I could no longer stand up to preach, so I ministered while sitting on a stool. I was referred to an oncologist at UCLA medical center in Los

Angeles. Over the next few weeks a series of tests were done, culminating in a bone marrow aspiration.

I had been online investigating what bone marrow testing involved. I saw a few testimonies, all of which scared me. One woman said that the bone marrow aspiration gave her more pain than childbirth. When I went for the test my wife and I prayed that I would not experience pain. When the doctor came in to conduct the aspiration he had in his hand a long needle. Lying on my stomach and I grabbed the sides of the gurney and held on tight waiting for the intensity of pain. A few minutes passed. Then the doctor said, "That's it, Mr. Adams." I couldn't believe it. I never felt any pain when he did it. Glory to God!

About three months after the original diagnosis all the results of the tests came back. I remember the doctor coming in with three interns. They were all smiling broadly like Cheshire cats. He turned on a large screen which showed the results of the testing. Every test was negative! The tumors had disappeared and I was healed! God had given me a testimony which I speak and write about to this day. There is power in corporate prayer; the prayers of the church throughout those three months had been answered. I set the stool aside behind the pulpit as a reminder of what God had done.

There are three ways God answers prayer: either yes, no, or wait. When the answer is yes it may be in a form completely different than what we expected it to be. When the answer is no, we must remember that God knows what is best for us. When the answer is wait, we must ask God for perseverance without doubting. Above all, we must walk by faith and not by sight.

In the book of Malachi God invites believers to try Him by an act of obedience. In this case the obedience is giving to God. Malachi 3:10 says, "Bring all the tithes into the storehouse, that there may be food in My house, and *try Me* now in this, if I will not open for you the windows of heaven and pour out so much blessing that there will not be room enough to receive it." It is a kingdom principle that obedience leads to blessing, not just for yourself but also for all those around you. I have emphasized this in the church for years. God wants to pour out blessings! He is waiting for us to seek Him, trust Him and obey Him. The words of the hymn "Trust and obey, for there is no other way to be happy in Jesus but to trust and obey" is so true.

However, we must not obey God just to receive blessings. We must obey God because of who He is. He is God, and we are not. He knows everything, and we do not. We express our love for God by obeying Him. Jesus said in John 14:15, "If you love Me, keep my commandments." Of course, Jesus summarized all the commandments into just two, namely love God and love others. When we love others, even our enemies, it is a form of obedience that God loves and honors. The Bible says twice in 1 John 4 that God is love.

Sharing answered prayers within the body of Christ results in edification. When we see how the Lord has moved and blessed our brothers and sisters in Christ, it increases our faith. Setting aside a time for testimonies in any church setting is important in bringing about greater assurance of the power and presence of God in our midst. Greater faith can lead to greater boldness when we put legs to our faith. This is perhaps the greatest reason for not neglecting the gathering together of the people of God. Hebrews 10:24-25 says, "And let us consider one another in order to *stir up* love and good works, not forsaking the assembling of ourselves together, as is the manner of some, but exhorting one another, and so much the more as you see the Day approaching." We cannot *stir up* one another by watching a service online. Person to person contact is vital in the body of Christ. Attempting to be a lone ranger Christian will only lead to loneliness and a slow slipping away from the things of God. This is becoming more and more imperative because the "Day" with a capital D mentioned in verse 25 is getting closer and closer. The nearer we get to the day of the Lord's return, the more the enemy will attempt to divide the church. Covid-19 was used by the devil to separate brothers and sisters in Christ from each other. It caused many believers to drop out and closed many church doors. The word "exhorting" in verse 25 means "to emphatically urge or encourage toward action".[9] Iron sharpening iron within the body of Christ is the last thing that Satan wants to see. The devil hates testimonies about answered prayer and will try to prevent us from sharing them. We must not allow distractions and hindrances to keep us from encouraging each other. Proverbs 12:25 says, "Anxiety in the heart of man causes depression, but a good word makes it glad." When people come to church downcast, the Lord can use a good word from us to be the lifter of their head, especially if we have been in their shoes earlier in life.

Finally, answered prayers facilitate unity. We rejoice as a body when someone is healed by, provided for, protected by, or given guidance by the hand of God. One good result of social media and the internet is sharing across denominational barriers what God is doing. When men and women of God gather together from various church families to share common experiences of answered prayer, the oneness that Jesus so greatly desires in the last days is facilitated.

CHAPTER 5

The Fulfillment of Prophecy

The dictionary definition of prophecy is "a statement that something will happen in the future". The biblical definition of prophecy is "something that God said will happen in the future". In the Bible God often used prophets to speak His words. 2 Peter 1:21 says, "for prophecy never came by the will of man, but holy men of God spoke as they were moved by the Holy Spirit."

In the Bible there are many prophecies that point to the first coming of Jesus; some scholars have estimated that there are over 300 such prophetic passages in the Old Testament.[10] These prophecies were fulfilled through the birth, life, death and resurrection of Jesus. There are many more prophecies which point to the second coming of Christ. It is estimated that there are at least 1,845 such prophetic scriptures, spanning both the Old Testament and the New Testament.[11] Thus there are approximately six times as many scriptures pointing to the second coming of Christ than there are pointing to His first coming to earth. This fact alone should demonstrate the paramount significance of this future event. It should impact the way we live as Christians as we anticipate His glorious appearing.

The fact that every prophetic scripture pointing to the Messiah's first coming was fulfilled in perfection to the smallest detail should be a testament to the supernatural accuracy of the Bible. It is the only book in all the world that foretells the future as it unfolds in front of our very eyes. It is divinely inspired, and much of it is written by and through prophets led by the Holy Spirit.

The word "redeem" is first mentioned in the Bible in the prophetic scripture Exodus 6:6, "Therefore say to the children of Israel: 'I am the Lord; I will bring you out from under the burdens of the Egyptians. I will rescue you from their bondage, and I will *redeem* you with an outstretched arm and with great judgments.'" This scripture points to the Passover and the deliverance of the Israelites as God's chosen people from the bondage of the Egyptians, an event yet to happen at the time the scripture was written. Many other prophetic scriptures point to the *redemption* of those who put their faith in God. The ultimate Redeemer, of course, is the Lord Jesus Christ, who, through His shed blood on the cross, delivered us from the bondage of sin and death.

It is thought by many Bible scholars that the book of Job may be the oldest book in the Bible. Yet there we find one of the greatest prophetic passages probably written before any other. Job 19:25-27 says, "For I know that my Redeemer lives, and He shall stand at last on the earth; and after my skin is destroyed, this I know, that in my flesh I shall see God, whom I shall see for myself, and my eyes shall behold, and not another. How my heart yearns within me." One of the purposes of biblical prophesy is to create such a yearning in the hearts of all true followers of Christ. This yearning should then spur us on to obedience and running the race diligently to the end.

It is remarkable that Job refers to the Lord as his "Redeemer" when the concept of redemption was most likely not fully developed in his mind. Taking this passage in context we know that Job had experienced tremendous loss. His family and his livelihood had been taken away, and his health was at its worst. Undoubtedly he wanted to be delivered from his situation. He realized that only God could restore what had been lost. The word "Redeemer" could also be translated "Savior". He needed someone to save him, someone to "buy him back" from his dire circumstances. Based on verse 26 and the phrase "after my skin is destroyed", Job must have believed in the resurrection of his body. So whether Job hoped for deliverance in this life or in the next, he had the assurance of *certain redemption* one way or another. This assurance was planted in his heart many centuries before the ultimate Redeemer came to the earth.

Psalm 130:7-8 says, "O Israel, hope in the Lord; for with the Lord there is mercy, and with Him is *abundant redemption*. And He shall *redeem* Israel from all his iniquities." This prophetic scripture first of all points to when God would *redeem* the Israelites from bondage in Babylon. But more than that it also looks forward to a time when God would *redeem* all true believers from slavery to their own sinful natures. This would be accomplished through the death and resurrection of Jesus Christ.

A foreshadowing of the *redemption* of God's people from sin is also found in the New Testament in the prophecy of Zacharias, the father of John the Baptist, in Luke 1:67-79. Verses 67-68 say, "Now his father Zacharias was filled with the Holy Spirit, and prophesied, saying: 'Blessed is the Lord God of Israel, for He has visited and *redeemed* His people,'". The presence of the Holy Spirit prompted Zacharias to announce God's promise of *redemption* from sin through Jesus Christ who was about to be born. This prophecy is given in the past tense, as if it had already occurred, because in the mind and heart of God it was already a *certainty* for those who would follow Jesus wholeheartedly.

One of the most assuring and comforting passages pointing prophetically to the second coming of Christ is found in the Old Testament in Isaiah 51:10-11, which says, "Are You not the One who dried up the sea, the waters of the great deep; that made the depths of the sea a road for the *redeemed* to cross over? So the *ransomed* of the Lord shall return, and come to Zion with singing, with everlasting joy on their heads. They shall obtain joy and gladness; sorrow and sighing shall flee away." This prophetic passage compares the crossing of the Red Sea on dry ground during the exodus to the return to Jerusalem of Jesus with all those who were bought back by Him because of their surrendered faithfulness to Him. To the truly surrendered follower of Christ this is a tremendous affirmation of *certain redemption* and the hope of being with Jesus in Jerusalem when He returns to earth in the future.

These passages are only a few of hundreds, both Old Testament and New Testament, which announce that Jesus is coming back. The fulfillment of prophetic passages in the Old Testament about the coming Messiah is proof that God is real, He is not hidden, and future events are laid out in detail in the Bible. If the unbeliever would have an open and willing heart to research the scriptures, the evidence of their supernatural forecasting of history is undeniable. This evidence leads to the conclusion that not only is the Bible written by God, but also that God is in control of history.

CHAPTER 6

Creation Itself

The Bible clearly states that men and women who question the existence of God are without excuse because the world and everything in it points to the reality of the Creator. Romans 1:20 says, "For since the creation of the world His invisible attributes are clearly seen, being understood by the things that are made, even His eternal power and Godhead, so that they are without excuse". There are so many natural phenomena that display the fingerprints of a Creator of all things. Among them are the growth of cells in living organisms, including our own bodies, the perfect placement of the earth in its orbit around the sun, and the hydrologic cycle of the continuous movement and interchange of water from clouds to rain to rivers to evaporation and back again to clouds. Only the most doubting skeptic could possibly believe that these things just happened to occur out of nothing.

The advancement of science has in many ways been a confirmation of the existence of God. For example, astronomy has revealed the uniqueness of planet earth in the vast universe, the only place known to sustain human life. It has been proven by science that if the orbit of the earth were only a few thousand miles closer to the sun, life would not be sustainable due to heat, and vice versa, if the orbit was farther away from the sun even a small amount, the earth would freeze. Only the Creator of the universe could have placed our world in such a perfect yearly cycle. The chances of it happening randomly are millions to one.

The uniqueness of each and every human being has also been proven by science with the discovery of DNA. Long before the discovery of the makeup and multiplication of cells, the Bible confirmed the distinctive individuality of each of us. David writes about the formation by God of each person from conception. In Psalm 139:16 he writes, "Your eyes saw my substance, being yet unformed. And in Your book they were all written, the days fashioned for me, when as yet there were none of them." No two men or women have ever been created identical. DNA reveals the incredible tiny detail that the Creator makes to create unique individuality. Even the fingerprints of any two persons are never exactly the same. Randomness cannot explain such detail.

Psalm 19:1-4 says, "The heavens declare the glory of God; and the firmament shows His handiwork. Day unto day utters speech, and night unto night reveals knowledge. There is no speech nor language where their voice is not heard. Their line has gone out through all the earth, and their words to the end of the world." The revelation of the created work of God in nature crosses all cultural and linguistic barriers. The mountains and oceans bear as much witness to the majesty and glory of God in China and Africa as they do in America. No one can be excused for denying the existence of God because we are surrounded by it wherever we look.

In addition, the Bible says in Ecclesiastes 3:11 that God has put eternity in the hearts of men. Humanity was created for eternity, which leads to a longing for something beyond this world.[12] The desire for something more than this world reflects the fact that man was created in the image of the eternal God. God does not hide Himself even from unrighteous men and women who continue to deny the existence of God even though it is evident all around them and even within them. Psalm 14:1 says, "The fool has said in his heart, 'There is no God.'" These same words are repeated by David again in Psalm 53:1, emphasizing the foolishness of believing that God is not real.

Another theme woven throughout scripture is the fact that creation became *corrupted* by the fall of man and the entrance of sin. Even that *corruption* bears witness to the presence of God in a fallen world. When Adam and Eve sinned in the Garden of Eden, the consequence was death. The Bible says the wages of sin is death, and now that is what men and women would eventually experience. Genesis 3:19 says, "In the sweat of your face you shall eat bread till you return to the ground, for out of it you were taken; for dust you are, and to dust you shall return." As a result of sin, our bodies are now subject to *corruption* and the aging process. In the previous verse we read that not only did mankind become corrupted by sin, but creation itself also became *corrupted*. In verses 17 and 18 we read, "…Cursed is the ground for your sake; in toil you shall eat of it all the days of your life. Both thorns and thistles it shall bring forth for you…" Not only has mankind experienced the *corruption* of being born with the sin nature, but all of creation is under the curse of sin which leads ultimately to death. All the earth and everything in it is now subject to *decay*, including plants and animals. Even inanimate objects left for many years will become corrupted and start to decay. An abandoned car left to the elements will rust and slowly fall apart. No part of God's beautiful creation is exempt from the result of rebellion against the Creator.

As we grow older and see the deterioration of our bodies over time, we can start to long for freedom from the effects of sin. We desire in greater measure the deliverance from corruption and decay. Unbelievers become trapped in bodies with no hope beyond their inevitable death. However, for true followers of Christ, we begin to long for new bodies promised us in 1 Corinthians 15 and the *certain redemption* that lies ahead. Romans 8:23 says, "…we also who have the firstfruits of the Spirit, even we ourselves *groan* within ourselves, *eagerly waiting* for the adoption, the *redemption* of our body."

The scripture also tells us that creation is also longing for the curse upon the earth to be lifted when Jesus comes back. Romans 8:19-22 says, "For the earnest expectation of the creation *eagerly waits* for the revealing of the sons of God. For the creation was subjected to futility, not willingly, but because of Him who subjected it in hope; because the creation itself also will be delivered from the *bondage of corruption* into the glorious liberty of the children of God. For we know that the whole creation *groans* and labors with birth pangs together until now." Mankind, animals, plants and all the earth wait eagerly for the end of the *bondage of corruption*. When Jesus rode on the donkey into Jerusalem on Palm Sunday, the disciples and the crowd were hailing Him as the long-awaited Messiah. The Pharisees called to Him to rebuke His disciples. Jesus replied that if the people were to remain silent, then the rocks would cry out. There is no part of God's creation that will not be delivered from the bondage that sin has brought about. Creation itself cries out for the *certain redemption* of mankind from the power of sin and death.

Finally, the Bible is full of examples of God's control of nature itself. Jesus revealed His omnipotence by calming the wind and the waves on the Sea of Galilee. The disciples in astonishment asked, "Who is this, that even the wind and the waves obey Him?" In the Old Testament, God parted the waters of the Red Sea and later the Jordan River, so that His people could walk through on dry ground. At one point God caused the sun to stand still. God sent fire from heaven to destroy the cities of Sodom and Gomorrah. Jesus multiplied loaves and fishes to feed thousands of people. The death of Jesus on the cross caused darkness to fall over the land in the middle of the day and an earthquake to occur. All these examples merely foreshadow what God will do in the future when he makes a new heaven and a new earth, the final home for all those truly surrendered to Christ. All of creation will be restored to its pristine state as it was before sin and death entered the world, and the *certain redemption* of true believers will be completed in that glorious place.

CHAPTER 7

Redemptive Analogies

One of the greatest pieces of evidence of not only the existence of God but also of His plan of *redemption* is found in *redemptive analogies*. It is unfortunate that many Christians have never heard of *redemptive analogies* and do not know what they are. Defining *redemptive analogies* takes us back to the Book of Genesis chapter 11. During the ten generations from Noah to Abraham pride had crept into the culture. The whole earth had one language. Verse 4 tells us the people said, "let us *make a name* for ourselves by building a tower which can reach to the heavens. The people had disobeyed the Lord's command in Genesis 9:1 to "fill the earth". They had settled in one area and become united for a sinful purpose, exalting themselves more than God. As a result, God came down, confused their language and *scattered* them over the face of the earth.

When God brings judgment on His people, He always has ultimate restoration and *redemption* in mind. God would now choose one people as His own, through Abraham, with the final goal of winning all the other people groups back unto Himself. God always *scatters* with the end goal of *regathering*. There are other biblical examples of when God scatters to accomplish His purpose of ultimate unity. When the disciples stayed in Jerusalem as a holy huddle after Pentecost, He allowed persecution to scatter them back into obedience to His command in Acts 1:8 to "be witnesses to Me in Jerusalem, and in all Judea and Samaria, and to the end of the earth." He even chose one of the elders from Acts 6:5, namely Philip, to be the first one to go to Samaria. Afterward He sent him to Gaza for his divine appointment with the Ethiopian eunuch, and then from there to Caesarea Phillipi where in Acts 21:8 he is seen continuing to evangelize. When we are unwilling, God will find and use someone who is willing. What God broke into pieces at the Tower of Babel was ultimately put back together in the Book of Acts. The unity God scattered at Babel was restored by grace on the Day of Pentecost. On that day people from all over the known world came together to hear the gospel in their own languages.[13] The unity which God ended at Babel was restored through the fledgling church and the resulting spread of the gospel of Jesus Christ in the first century.

After the scattering at the Tower of Babel, various people groups and nationalities became established with unique cultural differences. Because God always goes before us to prepare the way, He established within each of these people groups cultural traditions, ingrained behaviors, symbols and even alphabets which pointed to Jesus Christ as Savior of the world. He did this to facilitate the spread of the Gospel which would occur many centuries later. These cultural analogies pointed to the cross and the completed work of Christ. Therefore, the definition of a *redemptive analogy* is a cultural practice, custom, tradition or symbol planted by God within a people group pointing to the need for salvation through Jesus Christ.

Redemptive analogies also reflect the sovereignty of God in history. The preincarnate heart of God prepared the way for the work of His Son on the cross. God took the uniqueness of each culture which was established after the scattering at Babel and used it to later lead millions to faith in Christ. He also did this to further unveil the reality of His presence to those who would come to understand the amazing nature of these analogies.

Perhaps the most famous *redemptive analogy* is the "peace child" discovered by Don Richardson among the Sawi indigenous people of Papua, New Guinea. In his book "Peace Child" Richardson describes how the tribes were in constant conflict with each other.[14] Richardson and his family became fearful due to this warfare and decided to leave. To prevent them from leaving, the Sawi tribe and their enemy tribe came together to make peace. In their culture God had planted the concept of exchanging a young child as a peace offering. The opposing tribe would then care for the child as one of their own. This ritual reflected God giving His own Son to humanity to bring peace between God and mankind. This analogy was then used to win many souls to Christ in the Sawi culture.

Many people groups worldwide have as a central part of their religious practices the blood sacrifice of animals. We must not ignore this fact in attempting to evangelize these cultures. The Old Testament method for the remission of sin included animal sacrifice. This, of course, was replaced by the ultimate and final sacrifice of Jesus Christ on the cross for the atonement of sin. God Himself in human form paid the price in full for all sin. Belief in that sacrifice and surrender to God leads to salvation. Animal sacrifice under the law ended the day Christ died for us. In the process of sharing the gospel with people groups which already have animal blood sacrifice as a method of cleansing and purifying the person, it must be remembered that it is ultimately God who planted the idea of these practices in the hearts of the people. Leviticus 17:11 says, "For the life of the flesh is in the blood, and I have given it to you upon the altar to make atonement for your souls; for it is the blood that makes atonement for the soul." It is unlikely that the understanding of "the life is in the blood" came from pagan hearts and minds. It is likely that God took the words of Leviticus 17:11 and used them as a *redemptive analogy* to be a bridge when missionaries came evangelizing the people.

A good example of this can be found in the efforts to evangelize the Pokot tribe of Northern Kenya.[15] When pioneer missionaries first came to this tribe during the 1970's they ignored the practice of animal sacrifice in their culture. The missionaries tried to teach the people that their existing pagan religion was without any meaning. This turned many of the Pokot away from accepting Christ. Once the method of evangelization was changed, and existing practices began to be used as a link to sharing the gospel, many Pokot surrendered to Christ. It is important when missionary work is being done in whatever culture to remember two vital things. First, God has gone before us in every people group and culture to lay the groundwork for the truth of the gospel to be shared. Secondly, as it says in Ecclesiastes 3:11 God "has put eternity in their hearts". Every people group will be trying to fill the God-sized hole in the heart of every individual in some manner that will bring ultimate fulfillment. Only Christ can bring that fulfillment, and God has prepared the way in advance for that to take place through *redemptive analogies.*

Another powerful example of a *redemptive analogy* is found in the Sukuma ethnic group in Western Tanzania. Within this culture there is found the ritual of a sacrificial goat being killed "facing the eastern side of the universe".[16] The significance of facing *east* will be discussed further in a later chapter of this book. A spear is driven into the left fore-chest of the goat, careful not to pierce its heart. An English translation of the Sukuma proverb related to this ceremony is as follows: "The sacrificial goat dies while screaming in anguish." The goat's death is symbolic of restoration of the power of medicine used by the Sukuma "medicine man" or divine-healer, and the peace that comes to the people as a result.

The comparisons in this ceremony to the sacrifice of Jesus on the cross are striking. First the goat had to be pure white, representing innocence. Jesus was the perfect and pure Lamb of God. Secondly, the spear used to kill the goat did not pierce its heart, but only its side. The side of Jesus was pierced, according to the Bible, with "blood and water flowing out". Thirdly, just as the goat screams in anguish, so Jesus also cried out in anguish from the cross during His suffering. In addition, both the goat and Jesus were sacrificed publicly, and both died, the difference being that Jesus rose from the dead. This ritual can clearly be seen as a preparation for the arrival of the Gospel. It was placed in this people group by God centuries earlier.

Even symbols for letters or words can be seen as *redemptive analogies*. The Chinese symbol for *redemption*, for example, contains as part of it an easily identifiable cross. There are many other examples of *redemptive analogies* which are beyond the scope of this book.

Two significant conclusions can be brought about from recognizing *redemptive analogies* as God's way of making Himself real to a lost and dying world. One deduction is that God never wants to make Himself hidden. Even in bringing about *scattering* and judgment, God made a way for the truth of who He is to be known. His great love for humanity is revealed through providing spiritual arrows pointing clearly to the Gospel and the need for salvation. Another takeaway is God's omniscience, knowing the end from the beginning, and His desire to always have a clear pathway leading to *certain redemption* for anyone who truly believes and follows Him wholeheartedly.

CHAPTER 8

The Historical Record

When I was in the 10th grade in high school I took a World History class. The textbook for the course began with a history of ancient Egypt and progressed gradually forward in time to the advent of Christendom. It then covered the spread of Christianity throughout Europe leading up to the Renaissance and the Reformation, and then ultimately to the discovery of America. What I distinctly remember from that course were the many references in that textbook to the Bible, and how Christ seemed to be central to all of world history. This fact irked me at the time because I had become so turned off on religion and the Bible. However, years later, looking back as a believer, I remember how the Bible and world history are intertwined, and how leaving Jesus out of the historical record would be virtually impossible if the course was taught accurately.

The question that often arises regarding the Bible is whether it can be read and relied on as a completely accurate historical account or not. If it can be read as a history textbook as well as an object of faith, then history and faith become interwoven. The events depicted in the Bible then become historical proofs that God is not hidden. The truth about God contained in the events in the Bible that have already taken place then provide a secure foundation for believing the events in the future which are predicted, including the *certain redemption* of all true followers of Jesus Christ.

There are many proofs that the Bible is historically accurate to the smallest detail. Whereas historical texts other than the Bible are often filled with inconsistencies and inaccuracies, the Bible stands out as a totally reliable historical document.[17] In examining the evidence for this, it is important to remember that much of the Bible is not written in chronological order. The arrangement of the books in the Bible serves a purpose beyond mere chronology.[18] The order of the books provides a roadmap for understanding God's redemptive plan. While the placement of each book in the closed canon was determined by men, the perfection of the completed work testifies to the divine leading of the Holy Spirit in determining their order.

In comparing the historical record to the Bible, the years in which each book was written must be kept in mind. For example, much of the history found in 1 and 2 Samuel and 1 and 2 Kings is repeated in 1 and 2 Chronicles. However, 1 and 2 Chronicles was written more than 400 years after 1 and 2 Samuel and to a different audience. While the purpose of 1 and 2 Samuel recorded the national and political history of Israel leading up to God's judgment and their exile, the books of 1 and 2 Chronicles were written looking back spiritually at what happened leading up to those events. Believed to have been written by Ezra the priest, the Chronicles books had the purpose of reassuring the returning exiles from Babylon of the immutability of the promises of God.[19] Chronologically, the book of 2 Chronicles was one of the last books written in the Old Testament, probably written during the time of the prophet Malachi.

The Major Prophets, including Isaiah, Jeremiah and Ezekiel were pre-exilic, meaning they were written prior the exile. They lived during the historical period recorded in 1 and 2 Samuel and 1 and 2 Kings. The book of Daniel was written *during* the exile. While most of the Minor Prophets were pre-exilic, Haggai, Zechariah and Malachi were post-exilic and lived during the historical period recorded in Ezra and Nehemiah. It is important to realize that generations pass and much change occurs historically, even in a seventy year period.

Even though the Book of Job is placed after all the other historical books and right before Psalms in the Old Testament, the author and timeline of the book is basically unknown. Because of the locations referred to in Job, it has been suggested that Job may have lived after the scattering at the Tower of Babel and before the calling of Abraham somewhere around Genesis chapter 11.

In addition to this, Paul's letters in the New Testament are not included in chronological order. Written over a period of approximately 18 years from 50-52 A.D. to 66-68 A.D., the letters are distributed in the Bible by length and by targeted audience. The longest letters, Romans and 1 and 2 Corinthians are listed first with the shorter letters to follow.

As Paul traveled on his missionary journeys and established churches, he followed up by writing to them depending on what issues were developing. A chart by timeline, church and topic may be found in the article "New Testament Pauline Letters Chronological Order by Paul J. Bucknell published in Biblical Foundations For Freedom."[20]

There are many other historical writings and documents that expand on what is written in the Bible. What is remarkable is that these writings do not contradict or disprove any historical person, action, or location mentioned in Scripture. On the contrary, as more and more archeological and anthropological evidence has been accumulated over the past 150 years, inaccuracies in other historical literary works have far outnumbered any findings that might draw into question the accuracy of the Bible.

For example, the actual existence of King David was questioned for centuries, leading to his reign being thought of in secular circles as only a myth. Then in 1994 archeologists discovered a stone in northern Galilee with inscriptions referring to King David and the House of David.

Bible critics years ago cited no evidence for the existence of the Hittite people which are mentioned around 40 times in the Bible. In 1906 an archeologist in Turkey uncovered the capital city of the Hittite empire, including 10,000 clay tablets documenting Hittite history.[21]

The accuracy of the Book of Acts has also been brought into question. After 30 years of archeological research in the Middle East, the great historical scholar Sir William Ramsay stated that he found not one historical or geographical mistake by Luke in writing the Book of Acts, even though Luke mentions 32 countries, 54 cities, nine Mediterranean islands, and 95 people.[22]

More recent discoveries include an anchor found off the coast of Malta in 2005, known as "Benedict's Anchor" because it was located on the day that Pope Benedict XVI celebrated his first mass as pope. Five other anchors were previously hoisted from the sea depths on the north shore of Malta in the 1960's and 1980's.[23] It is believed by many archeologists that among these are the four anchors jettisoned from the ship that carried the Apostle Paul when he was shipwrecked on the island of Malta on the way to Rome. Acts 27:29 reads, "Then, fearing lest we should run aground on the rocks, they dropped four anchors from the stern and prayed for day to come." Verse 40 reads, "And they let go the anchors and left them in the sea…"

In the same year 2005 the Pool of Siloam in Jerusalem was uncovered in an archeological find. In John 9:7and 9:11 a blind man who had been anointed by Jesus went and washed in the Pool of Siloam and received his sight. Another much earlier archeological excavation in 1956 revealed the Pool of Bethesda where in John 5:2-4 Jesus healed the man who had been paralyzed for 38 years.

Secular historical documents also support the accuracy of Scripture. The Roman historian Tacitus, whose writings are dated from 115 A.D., in mentioning the problems created by Christians in Rome, wrote, "They got their name from Christ, who was executed by sentence of the procurator Pontius Pilate in the reign of Tiberius".[24]

Regarding the Old Testament, it was once believed that through many centuries the writings would have been altered, changed or corrupted. The discovery of the Dead Sea Scrolls in 1947 changed all that. Every book of the Old Testament except Esther was contained in these scrolls. Found in caves on the northwestern shore of the Dead Sea, they have been carbon dated to have been written somewhere between 200 BC and 100 BC. Prior to then the oldest complete copy of the Old Testament was dated around 900 AD. The comparison between the two was striking, the scriptures being nearly identical. The Smithsonian Institute has stated, "the historical books of the Old Testament are as accurate as any that we have from antiquity and are in fact more accurate than many of the Egyptian, Mesopotamian, or Greek histories".[25]

There are many more historical documents and archeological finds that provide proof of the accuracy of the Bible, much more than can be contained in this book. Suffice it to say that the reliability of the Bible as historically accurate serves as an anchor for the faith of all true believers. The Bible stands alone as a record of both past history and future events. We can be assured that every future historical event in the Bible will happen precisely as it is written, including the *certain redemption* of all true followers of Jesus Christ.

CHAPTER 9

The Jewish Wedding

As followers of Christ, we await the return of the Bridegroom to take His bride home. The Bridegroom is Jesus and the bride is His church. This is an analogy that is repeated in various ways in Scripture. In Matthew 22:1-14 we find what is known as the Parable of the Wedding Feast. This parable emphasizes the importance of accepting the invitation to the feast, as well as the fact that no one can attend the feast without wearing a wedding garment. The invitation is symbolic of accepting Jesus into our hearts as Lord and Savior. The wedding garment is the righteousness of Christ which is ours once we surrender to Jesus and follow Him. These are the surface truths we obtain from the parable. However, there is much, much more to unpack from this parable.

Weddings are joyous occasions in the present time, and the same was true when Jesus spoke this parable. However, the wedding Jesus describes was totally different from modern-day weddings, including different from Jewish weddings celebrated today. Ancient Jewish weddings never involved a wedding ceremony like we see today with the bride walking down the aisle in the synagogue. The modern ceremony did not develop until hundreds of years after Jesus rose from the dead.

The wedding Jesus refers to in this parable is not a "wedding ceremony", but rather a "wedding feast". A wedding feast in the time of Jesus was the last step in a series of steps in a marriage process that took months, sometimes even years.[26] There were three stages in a Jewish marriage in the first century. These were the contract, the consummation and the celebration. In modern-day weddings, consummation is the last thing that takes place when the couple comes together physically in what we call the honeymoon. In the wedding in the time of Jesus, the consummation had already taken place before the wedding feast. As will become clear, this holds great significance as far it relates to the analogy of Christ and His church.

First of all, the marriage contract was accomplished in seven steps. The first of these steps was the selection of the bride. In ancient Israel, brides were usually chosen by the father of the bridegroom. He would send his most trusted servant to search for a bride for his son. Even if the groom and bride were ultimately involved in the selection process themselves, the final decision about the marriage was always made by the father of the bridegroom. In Matthew 22:2 Jesus begins the parable with these words, "The kingdom of heaven is like a certain king who *arranged* a marriage for his son".

It has been *arranged* in the heart of God from eternity past to provide a bride for His Son, Jesus Christ. God the Father and Jesus Christ, being one with each other within the Godhead, chose us to be the bride of Christ. In John 15:16 Jesus said, "You did not choose Me, but I chose you and appointed you that you should go and bear fruit, and that your fruit should remain". The fruit of a marriage is offspring, and the fruit of our marriage with Christ is many more souls won to Jesus.

Often the bride did not even see the groom until the consummation of the marriage contract. We have not physically seen Jesus, but God has revealed Him to us by the Holy Spirit. 1 Peter 1:8 says, "whom having not seen you love. Though now you do not see Him, yet believing, you rejoice with joy inexpressible and full of glory".

The second step in a Jewish marriage contract in the days of Jesus was payment of the price for the bride. Brides in the time of Jesus were purchased. The price was paid to the father of the bride, both to compensate him for the loss of the worker and to show how much the bridegroom loved and cherished the bride. We, as the bride of Christ, have also been purchased or *redeemed* with a price, namely the blood of Jesus shed on the cross to pay for our sins. 1 Peter 1:18-19 says, "knowing that you were not redeemed with corruptible things, like silver or gold, from your aimless conduct received by tradition from your fathers, but with the precious blood of Christ, as of a lamb without blemish and without spot". The price paid for we the bride of Christ demonstrates how much Jesus as the bridegroom loves and cherishes us as His bride. Romans 5:8 says, "But God demonstrates His own love toward us, in that while we were still sinners, Christ died for us."

The third step in a marriage contract in the time of Jesus was the signing of the contract or *Ketubah*. This represented the actual betrothal of the bride to the bridegroom. The betrothal is much like our engagement contract today, but with a much greater sense of commitment. During the betrothal the couple is actually entering into a covenant. Covenant in Bible times was serious, final, sealed in blood and legally binding. Once a couple entered into the covenant of betrothal, they were legally married in all aspects except for the physical consummation of the marriage. The *Ketubah* consists of all the bridegroom's promises to his bride. The bride cherishes the *Ketubah*.

We, too, have a *Ketubah* from our Bridegroom. Our marriage contract is God's Word! Our *Ketubah* shows us all we are entitled to as the Bride of Christ. All, not some, but all the promises in God's Word, are for us. As the Bride of Christ, we are entitled to them. They are part of our *Ketubah*.

The fourth step in a Jewish marriage contract was the cup of the covenant. After the terms of the *Ketubah* were accepted, a cup of wine was shared to seal the marriage covenant. A *second cup* would be shared many months or even years later at the wedding feast when the bridegroom would return for his bride.

Jesus referred to His suffering on the cross as His "*cup*". In this context, His "cup" represented the sealing of the marriage covenant between Jesus and the church. It represented the *first cup*, which sealed for all true followers of Christ the forgiveness of sins through His shed blood on the cross. The covenant was sealed the moment Jesus said "It is finished!" and died in the place of sinners. This was the moment when God, in the person of the Bridegroom, sacrificed His life for His bride, the church. On that day the church was birthed into existence for all who would believe, even the thief on the cross who had just expressed his belief in Jesus.

At the last supper on the night Jesus was betrayed, "He took the *cup*, and gave thanks, and gave it to them, saying, 'Drink from it, all of you, for this is My blood of the new covenant, which is shed for many for the remission of sins.'" Later, in the Garden of Gethsemane, Jesus prayed, "Father, if you are willing, please take this *cup* away from Me; nevertheless not My will, but Yours, be done." Earlier in His ministry, when James and John were asking to sit on His right hand and left hand in His glory, Jesus said to them, "You do not know what you ask. Are you able to drink the *cup* that I drink, and be baptized with the baptism that I am baptized with?" Jesus repeatedly cast Himself in the role of Bridegroom by referring to the "*cup*" of His suffering which would seal the covenant of marriage with His bride, consisting of all truly surrendered believers.

At the closing of the last supper Jesus said, "But I say to you, I will not drink of this fruit of the vine from now on until that day when I drink it new with you in My Father's kingdom." This statement points to the *second cup* that we, the bride of Christ, will share with Him one glorious day at our wedding feast, known as the marriage supper of the Lamb.

The fifth step in a Jewish marriage contract was the departure of the bridegroom. Once the marriage contract was sealed, the bridegroom left to go to his father's house to prepare a wedding chamber. He would usually be gone many months, even up to seven years. The number seven is a very significant number in the Bible. We see the seven-year period in Genesis in the betrothal of Jacob and Leah and later Jacob and Rachel. God created the world in six days and rested on the seventh. The number seven points to completeness and divine perfection. The return of the Lord Jesus Christ to the earth as the Bridegroom will bring the divine perfection of His presence to our world.

In referring to His departure Jesus told the disciples in John 14:2-3, "In My Father's house are many mansions. If it were not so, I would have told you. I go to prepare a place for you. And if I go to prepare a place for you, I will come again and receive you to Myself, that where I am, there you may be also." Our Bridegroom has gone to prepare a wedding chamber for His bride the church.

The sixth step in a Jewish marriage contract was the return of the Bridegroom. Jewish bridegrooms usually came for their brides late at night, near the midnight hour. The sound of the shofar would break the silence of the night, and there would be great shouting and dancing in the streets. In the parable of the ten virgins in Matthew 25:6 it says, "And at midnight a cry was heard, 'Behold, the bridegroom is coming; go out to meet him!'"

As a thief in the night, Jesus as our Bridegroom will call us to arise and meet Him in the air. We will hear a shout and the sound of the shofar. It will happen quickly. We must be ready. Matthew 24:27 says, "For as the lightning comes from the east and flashes to the west, so also will the coming of the Son of Man be." 1 Thessalonians 4:16-18 says, "For the Lord Himself will descend from heaven with a shout, with the voice of an archangel, and with the trumpet of God. And the dead in Christ will rise first. Then we who are alive and remain shall be caught up together with them in the clouds to meet the Lord in the air. And thus we shall always be with the Lord. Therefore comfort one another with these words."

The seventh and final step in a Jewish marriage contract was known as the *huppah* or "hometaking", in which the bridegroom takes his bride to the bridal chamber. The word *huppah* originally meant consecrated room or holy covering. The *huppah* of ancient times was a special room built in the bridegroom's father's house. The room was usually replaced by a bridal canopy. The *huppah* symbolized the new house to which the bridegroom would take his bride. The bride and bridegroom were escorted to the bridal chamber where they would be alone for seven days. The spiritual parallel to the *huppah* for the bride of Christ begins as the church is lifted up off the earth to be taken to our heavenly wedding chamber where we will spend one week (seven years) with our Bridegroom. While the bride of Christ is in the bridal chamber with Jesus, the rest of the world will be in the seven-year tribulation. Isaiah 26:20-21 tells us of this time, "Come, my people, enter your chambers, and shut your doors behind you; hide yourself, as it were, for a little moment, until the indignation is past. For behold, the Lord comes out of His place to punish the inhabitants of the earth for their iniquity". While the wrath of God is poured out on the earth, the bride of Christ will be hidden away with her Bridegroom.

Before the bride could be taken to the bridal chamber and consummation could take place, the bride had to be proved pure. To confirm her virginity two elderly women were often called upon to do a physical inspection of her vagina to confirm that the hymen had not yet been broken. Even then, after consummation took place, a "virginity cloth" was brought before the elders to verify that the hymen had been broken during initial intercourse. The blood on the sheet or cloth provided proof of purity. If the bride is proved unpure, the consequences could be deadly. If evidence of impurity due to promiscuity is found and reported by the bridegroom the law in Deuteronomy 22:21 provided, "then they shall bring the young woman to the door of her father's house, and the men of her city shall stone her to death with stones, because she has done a disgraceful thing in Israel, to play the harlot in her father's house. So you shall put away the evil from among you." Once consummation had taken place, and the bride was proved to be pure, then the celebration could start, and the wedding feast could take place.

In the Jewish marriage the bride had to be proved pure, unstained and untarnished. The church today, as the bride of Christ, when we are all taken to the bridal chamber in heaven which Jesus the Bridegroom has prepared for us, will already have been proved pure through the atoning sacrifice and shed blood of Jesus on the cross. The righteousness of Christ will be upon all truly surrendered believers. The question of purity and holiness in the sight of God will already have been settled. There will be no question about the purity of the bride. 2 Corinthians 5:21 says, "For He made Him who knew no sin to be sin for us, that we might become the righteousness of God in Him."

At the end of seven days in the bridal chamber, the bridegroom and his bride would go to the marriage feast where there would be great joy, music and dancing. The wedding feast in Matthew 22 represents the marriage supper of the Lamb described in Revelation 19:6-9, "And I heard, as it were, the voice of a great multitude, as the sound of many waters and as the sound of mighty thunderings, saying, 'Alleluia! For the Lord God Omnipotent reigns!' Let us be glad and rejoice and give Him glory, for the marriage of the Lamb has come, and His wife has made herself ready. And to her it was granted to be arrayed in fine linen, clean and bright, for the fine linen is the righteous acts of the saints. Then he said to me, 'Write: 'Blessed are those who are called to the marriage supper of the Lamb!'' And he said to me, 'These are the true sayings of God.'" We as truly surrendered followers of Jesus will be dressed in fine linen, clean and bright, not because of anything we ever have done but only because of what Jesus did on the cross. His shed blood erased our sins and made us worthy in the sight of God, because the righteousness of Christ is upon us. The righteousness of Christ is our *wedding garment.*

In the parable of the wedding feast in Matthew 22:11 the king found a man at the feast who did not have on a wedding garment. That man was taken and thrown out of the feast. Not only that, he was bound hand and foot, taken away, and cast into outer darkness where there will be weeping and gnashing of teeth. This man represents those who say they are Christians but are not truly surrendered to Christ. Pretending to be something that you are not is the definition of hypocrisy. That is precisely what Jesus was accusing the Pharisees of. Many are called to the wedding feast, but only true followers of Christ wear the wedding garment.

In the movie "Wedding Crashers" a couple of con men keep getting away with attending wedding celebrations to which they have never been invited. They look the part and try to blend in but eventually they get caught and thrown out. No one will be able to crash the wedding feast of the Lamb. In the parable those at the feast did not notice the difference in dress, but the king did. Jesus knows His sheep, and only they will be present at the marriage supper of the Lamb. The practical application from the parable is to put off pretense, and truly follow Jesus. A person cannot put on a wedding garment in church on Sunday, and then go home and put on filthy rags the rest of the week. Jesus is either Lord of all or Lord not at all.

There are many analogies between Jewish weddings during the first century and the marriage of Christ and His church. These analogies scream the fact that God is not hidden, but rather has made Himself known through history and culture as they relate to His Word. Jeremiah 29:13 says,

"And you will seek Me and find Me, when you search for Me with all your heart." Certainly culture and history during the ministry of Jesus on the earth in the first century confirm that *certain redemption* awaits only those believers who are truly surrendered to God.

CHAPTER 10

East vs. West and the Spread of the Gospel

Everything in all creation points to the truth of Scripture, including *geography* as well as history and culture. Even a map of the world and the way the Gospel of Jesus Christ was shared and spread from continent to continent points to the existence of our Creator. From the birth of cartography to the discovery of America as an eventual springboard for missionaries, the master design of the world as we know it today began in the mind and heart of Almighty God. An exploration of the significance of the design of the earth and the way geography supports the reality of God and the truth of the Bible must begin with *directions* and *orientation*. The four directions, namely east, west, north and south all hold implications regarding spiritual truth.

Perhaps the greatest understanding of the heart of God regarding *sin* comes from the significance of east vs. west in the Bible. The word *east* or *eastward* is mentioned at least 80 times in Scripture, depending on the translation, whereas the word *west* or *westward* has 55 or more references. The scriptural evidence of moving in an *eastward* direction away from God and into sin is overwhelming. In contrast, moving *westward* implies moving toward God and away from sin. To move from *east* to *west* is to come back to His Presence. Both the tabernacle and later the temple were designed and set up that way. The first thing one would encounter when entering the tabernacle or the temple from the *east* was the altar of sacrifice for the forgiveness of sins. Next would come the basin of water for cleansing before entering the Holy Place.[27] While this metaphor cannot be applied dogmatically, many scriptures and Bible events support it.

Let's begin with Psalm 103:12 which says, "As far as the *east* is from the *west*, so far has He removed our transgressions from us." This verse tells us there is a great distance between these two directions. After all, the sun rises in the *east* and sets in the *west*, the opposite end of the horizon. But why is the *east* mentioned first as being *far*? Why does the scripture not say, "as far as the *west* is from the *east*? Notice how moving *east* to *west* coincides with the natural order of the day as created by God, whereas going from *west* to *east* is moving opposite the natural order of the day. In other words, *east* to *west* movement is in alignment with God's created order; *west* to *east* movement is in resistance to God's created order. Sin is resistance to God's created order, and this gives us the first scriptural confirmation of the analogy.

The beginning of the metaphor is found in the Garden of Eden. When Adam and Eve sinned, they were exiled *eastward* from the garden. Genesis 3:24 says, "So He drove out the man; and He placed cherubim at the *east* of the garden of Eden, and a flaming sword which turned every way, to guard the way to the tree of life." Later after Cain killed his brother Abel, he dwelled *east* of Eden. Genesis 4:16 says, "Then Cain went out from the presence of the Lord and dwelt in the land of Nod on the *east* of Eden." Notice that sin drove Cain "out from the presence of the Lord" in an *easterly* direction. The consequences of sin drove both Adam and Eve and their son Cain *eastward*. In the writing of Josephus in 93 A.D. entitled *Antiquities of the Jews*, it is speculated that Cain continued his wickedness in Nod, altering human culture into craftiness and deceit.[28] The land of Nod symbolizes wandering away from God and the condition of all who forsake God. The metaphor continues when the Lord led Abram to leave Ur of the Chaldeans and travel hundreds of miles to the land of Canaan. This is the first example in the Bible of *westward* migration since Israel (the land of Canaan) is located primarily *west* of Iraq (Ur of the Chaldeans). The obedience of Abram in traveling *east* to *west* is the first Biblical example of moving away from sin and toward God. On arriving in the Promised Land Abram built altars to the Lord and called on His name. In Genesis 12:8, it says, "And he moved from there to the mountain *east* of Bethel, and he pitched his tent with Bethel on the *west* and Ai on the *east*; there he built an altar to the Lord and called on the name of the Lord." According to Genesis 28:19 Bethel means "House of God". It is where Jacob later had the vision of a ladder reaching to heaven. On the other hand, the name Ai means "heap of ruins". Much later, in the book of

Joshua, it became the site of one of Israel's defeats because sin was found in the camp. Abram originally camped in the middle, halfway between the way of moving toward God and the way of moving away from God. This is symbolic of the decision we must make everyday as followers of Christ to either go His way or go our own.

After this Abram chose to go neither *east* nor *west*, but rather south into Egypt. There he got into a big mess by lying to Pharoah by saying that Sarai was his sister instead of his wife. He then returns to the place between Bethel and Ai. Meanwhile, both Abram and his nephew Lot become prosperous with so many livestock that they need to part ways to have enough land. Abram gave Lot the choice which direction he should go. Lot saw that the plain of the Jordan toward the *east* looked well-watered like the garden of the Lord. In Genesis 13:11-12 it says, "Then Lot chose for himself all the plain of Jordan, and Lot journeyed *east*. And they separated from each other. Abram dwelt in the land of Canaan, and Lot dwelt in the cities of the plain and pitched his tent even as far as Sodom." We know from Scripture that Lot got into all manner of troubles once he departed from Abram and the land of Canaan which God had called them to. First, he was captured by pagan kings and Abram had to fight them to rescue his nephew. Later two angels were sent by the Lord to rescue Lot and his family from the homosexual men of Sodom. Taking his eyes off the Lord and placing them on what pleased his eyes and benefited his livelihood brought consequences to Lot. Choosing to proceed *eastward* away from his uncle and the presence and protection of God was a mistake.

Before continuing it must be understood *geographically* what the *direction of the wilderness* refers to. The only lands which could be described as wilderness land lie either to the *east* or the *south* of Jerusalem. The largest wilderness *south* of Israel is found in the Sinai Peninsula where the Israelites wandered for forty years. Other lands referred to in the Bible which would be primarily *south* of Israel would include the Wilderness of Beersheba and the Wilderness of Paran, both mentioned in relation to where Hagar and Ishmael were sent when Abram cast them out. Some Bible scholars argue that the Wilderness of Paran where Ishmael later dwelt included the area *south* and *east* of the Dead Sea. The primary wilderness that is directly *east* of Jerusalem would be the land *east* of the Jordan River known as Moab which is now the modern-day country of Jordan. The distance from Jerusalem to Jericho is 18 miles with a drop in elevation of more than 3000 feet. There can be a difference in temperature of 20 to 30 degrees. Jerusalem sits in mountainous terrain, whereas Jericho, Moab and the Dead Sea are all hot, dry and below sea level. The most likely area referred to as *wilderness* in the Bible would be the land surrounding or just south of the Dead Sea, all of which is desert *wilderness* and is primarily *east* or *southeast* of Jerusalem.

In Leviticus chapter 16 the phrase "into the wilderness" is repeated three times in verses 10, 21 and 22, in relation to where the *scapegoat* would be sent away to and then released. It describes the wilderness as an *uninhabited land* in verse

22. The *scapegoat* was one of two goats commanded by the Lord to bear all the iniquities of the people. The first goat was sacrificed, and its blood was shed. The second goat, or *scapegoat*, would have all the transgressions of the children of Israel placed upon its head and sent out into the *wilderness*. Jewish tradition tells us that the distance between Jerusalem and the beginning of the *wilderness* is ninety stadia or approximately eleven miles. A man would escort the goat eleven miles and then release it. It is believed that these eleven miles were divided into ten intervals, and at the end of each of these intervals there was a station which offered refreshment for the man escorting the goat.[29] This was probably due to the increasing temperature in the descent and the lack of fresh water along the way. The point here is that the *direction of the wilderness* in this case had to be directly *east* of Jerusalem and toward the Dead Sea. The goat took the sins of the people *eastward* just as the sin of Cain was taken *eastward* and the sins of Adam and Eve were taken *eastward*.

Scripture tells us that the child Ishmael was conceived in iniquity with Hagar outside the covenant of faith, whereas the child Isaac was the son of promise conceived by Abraham and Sarah within the covenant of faith. The contrast between the two is addressed by the apostle Paul in the Book of Galatians 4:23, "But he who was of the bondwoman was born according to the flesh, and he of the freewoman through promise". It is believed that the descendants of Ishmael formed the beginning of the Arab people in what is now Saudi Arabia. The Arabian Peninsula lies both *south* and *east* of Israel. The sins of Abraham and Sarah in getting ahead of God and trying to produce the heir of promise with the handmaid Hagar resulted in the bondwoman and her son moving primarily *eastward*. Muslims believe that Muhammad was the descendant of Ishmael.[30] Ishmael is mentioned over ten times in the Quran. While there is no direct evidence that the other major *eastern* religions, such as Hinduism and Buddhism, developed from the lineage of Ishmael, it is nevertheless important to remember that Abraham and his father Terah lived in Mesopotamia, which is modern-day Iraq, before Abraham traveled to the land of Canaan. Both Hinduism and Buddhism are said to have their roots in India and Pakistan around 2000 to 1500 B.C. This is also roughly the same time during which Abraham and Ishmael lived. The point here is that all the religions based on false belief systems and false gods developed *east* of Israel. Hagar and Ishmael were released into the wilderness *eastward* just as the scapegoat was released into the wilderness *eastward*. The sins of Abraham and Sarah brought about consequences which have lasted for many centuries, even to the point of determining to a large extent the religious landscape of the world today. The enmity between the descendants of Isaac and Ishmael continue today in the form of the modern-day Arab-Israeli conflict. In referring to Ishmael the Bible says in Genesis 16:12, "He shall be a wild man; His hand shall be against every man, and every man's hand against him. And he shall dwell in the presence of all his brethren." When we see the unrestrained brutality and genocide associated with terrorist groups such as Hamas today it reminds us of the revelation of sin and its consequences after many generations.

There is also an illustration of this metaphor in the Book of Exodus when God sent the plague of locusts upon the land of Egypt. Exodus 10:13 tells us, "So Moses stretched out his rod over the land of Egypt, and Lord brought an *east* wind on the land all that day and all that night. When it was morning, the *east* wind brought the locusts. Once Pharoah confessed his sin, even though it was not genuine repentance, in Exodus 10:19 it says, "And the Lord turned a very strong *west* wind, which took the locusts away and blew them into the Red Sea. There remained not one locust in all the territory of Egypt." Deliverance for the Egyptians came from *west* to *east* and the fact that not one locust remained was symbolic of the all-encompassing completeness of the *redemption* which was accomplished for all truly surrendered believers through the blood of Jesus shed on the cross.

The next example of the metaphor is found in the Book of 2 Samuel when David fled from his son Absalom who was attempting to usurp the throne of the king. While God had forgiven David of the sin of adultery with Bathsheba and being responsible for the death of her husband Uriah, the consequences of those sins continued to plague King David, including the arrogance and betrayal of his own son Absalom. In fear for his life David fled Jerusalem *eastward*, crossing the Kidron Valley and climbing to the top of the Mount of Olives. 2 Samuel 15:23 says, "And all the country wept with a loud voice, and all the people crossed over. The king himself also crossed over the Brook Kidron, and all the people crossed over toward *the way of the wilderness*." Later in 2 Samuel 16:5 we find David at Bahurim, a village on the way down to the Jordan River. As Absalom pursued him, in 2 Samuel 17:24 David fled further *eastward*, crossing the Jordan River and staying at a village named Mahanaim in the land of Gilead *east* of the Jordan River. As a consequence of his earlier sin David fled *eastward* from Jerusalem. It was only after the death of his son Absalom that he was able to return *westward* back to Jerusalem.

All the above scriptural analogies are mere foreshadows of the movements of the Messiah, the Lord Jesus Christ, and his mission to conquer sin and death. We begin with the star of Bethlehem which moved from *east* to *west* and led the three wise men to the birthplace of Jesus. Matthew 2:9 says, "…and behold, the star which they had seen in the *east* went before them, till it came and stood over where the young Child was." The star and the magi traveled *east* to *west*, symbolizing and foreshadowing the conquering of sin which would be accomplished by the Savior. This *east* to *west* direction pointed the way to salvation through Christ.

Years later when Jesus entered Jerusalem riding on the colt in the triumphal entry, he traveled *east* to *west*, from the Mt. of Olives down the *crooked* path crossing the Brook Kidron and up into the city through the *eastern* gate and unto the Temple Mount. Though indeed He was King of Kings, he navigated the road on that donkey as the Lamb of God who came to pay for our sins. All the adulation He received as He entered Jerusalem He deserved even though His mission was misunderstood. The *east* to *west* route was *crooked*, representing the corrupted way of sin. He came as the sin-bearer that day. Only days later Jesus would travel *west* to *east*, down the Via Dolorosa, carrying the cross on which He would be crucified, to conquer sin through His shed blood. Yet all along Jesus knew this was not the first time He would traverse the path from the Mount of Olives into Jerusalem and the Temple Mount. He knew the scripture in Isaiah which prophesied the second time He would journey this way. Isaiah 40:4-5 says, "Every valley shall be exalted and every mountain and hill brought low; the *crooked* places shall be made *straight* and the rough places smooth; the glory of the Lord shall be revealed, and all flesh shall see it together; for the mouth of the Lord has spoken." He also knew what the scriptures said in Zechariah 14:4, "And in that day His feet will stand on the Mount of Olives, which faces Jerusalem on the *east*. And the Mount of Olives shall be split in two, from *east* to *west*, making a very large valley…" When Jesus traveled from the Mount of Olives into Jerusalem the first time, the *crooked* path of sin had not yet been conquered. That would be accomplished on the cross. However, the second time that Jesus will traverse that route, sin will already have been conquered. He will ride on a white stallion as King of Kings and Lord of Lords, having made the *crooked* places *straight*. In both cases His route is *east* to *west*, proclaiming Him as the Messiah who breaks the curse of sin and opens the door of salvation for all people.

There is a closed gate known as the *eastern* gate facing *east* in the wall around Jerusalem. Jesus is the only one who can open that gate because He has conquered sin once and for all on the cross. If you stand looking *westward* from the top of the Mount of Olives, you will see the *eastern* gate directly below the site of the Temple Mount. No prophetic scriptures could be clearer about the future coming of our Savior King to pass from *east* to *west* through that *eastern* gate than Ezekiel 43:1,2 and 4: "Afterward he brought me to the gate, the gate that faces toward the *east*. And behold, the glory of the God of Israel came from the way of the *east*." "And the glory of the Lord came into the temple by way of the gate which faces toward the *east*." That gate is currently shut because we still live in a sin-riddled world. Just as Jesus is the only one worthy enough to open the scroll in the Book of Revelation, He is also the only one worthy enough to open the *eastern* gate at His second coming, having gained victory over sin and the consequence of sin which is death.

Now let us return to the original premise of *eastward* movement being away from God and into sin and *westward* movement being toward God and away from sin, and then relate it to the church. In which direction did the Gospel primarily spread in the first century? Within Israel it spread north and south from Jerusalem. But in terms of worldwide spread it advanced mostly to the *west*. The missionary journeys of the apostle Paul to Asia Minor, Greece and eventually Rome were all *westward* in direction. Through the centuries afterward, the advancement of the church was north and *west* through the Germanic countries and eventually to France and England. Then the greatest *westward* movement of the Gospel occurred when it spread across the Atlantic to the Americas. Though it is challenged in secular circles today, history clearly teaches that the United States was founded as a Christian nation. As pioneers journeyed *westward* across the Mississippi and from there to California and the West, so did the church and the spread of the Gospel.

In contrast, the spread of the Gospel *eastward* from Jerusalem did not begin to take place until many centuries had passed. The founding of Islam, Hinduism and Buddhism, all of which are false religions, prevented it. The *way of the wilderness* and the consequences of the *eastern* march of sin and false teaching blocked it. Beginning in the nineteenth and twentieth centuries, missionaries started to make an impact in the nations of the *East*. Though the Gospel has spread *eastward* into Middle Eastern and Oriental countries, in many cases the church has had to go underground due to persecution. The consequences of sin have been far-reaching through the centuries.

The *geographical* layout of the world today is another confirmation of the reality of who God is, the consequences of sin, and the freedom that comes where the Gospel is welcome and the bondage that occurs where it is rejected.

CHAPTER 11

God's Patience and Sovereignty

We live in an age of instant gratification. We can get immediate answers to almost any question by googling it. Waiting in line for anything in our running to and fro society causes many to lose patience. The Bible makes a big deal about patience. It is listed as the fourth fruit of the Spirit in Galatians 5:22 right after love, joy and peace. Colossians 3:12 tells us to bear with one another with patience. We live in an age when patience seems to have become a lost art.

There is another word for patience in the Bible, and that word is *longsuffering*. If we break that word down in two parts, it basically means to *suffer long* for something or someone. Sometimes when many days, weeks, months or even years pass by, and we do not see anything happening, it can feel like suffering. But when we truly love someone, to suffer long for them and be patient with them can become a duty borne joyfully rather than a burden borne unwillingly.

Patience is a virtue especially important in marriage. This is facilitated by seeing things from the perspective of our spouse. Being patient becomes easier when self-focus is overcome. Two opposite personalities within a marriage can truly become one if the focus is on each other. For example, my wife Rosalie and I have opposite personalities. She is outgoing and perky whereas I am more introverted and reserved. I often say she lives in "fast forward" while I live in "slow motion". I call her *conejo* which in Spanish means rabbit whereas she refers to me as *tortuga* which is translated turtle. What has helped us immensely in our 42 years of marriage is my willingness to catch up with rabbit and her willingness to wait for turtle. God put us together because we complement one another. Above all, we are both led by the Holy Spirit which indwells us and helps us to see things from the perspective of our spouse. Being one with each other and one with Jesus should always be the goal in any equally yoked marriage. Much greater patience and *longsuffering* is required in an unequally yoked marriage. Prayer must be the foundation in such a case, first to facilitate patience on the part of the believing spouse, and most importantly to believe for the salvation of the unbelieving spouse. This type of patience may take years to see it happen. It is extremely unwise for any truly surrendered believer to enter into an unequally yoked marriage. True patience with each other comes only when God is at the heart of the union.

The patience of God as revealed in Scripture must be the example we follow as believers. After all, God has been patient in bringing about *certain redemption* for all truly surrendered believers from eternity past until now. His plan of salvation for mankind has been in process for thousands of years. One of the most irritating words when it comes to waiting is the word *delay*. To understand what looks to us as *delay*, we need to see things from God's perspective. We are just a tiny part of history, a vapor that is here and gone. We are limited in what we can see and know. God is not limited. This is best explained in Isaiah 55:8-9, "'For My thoughts are not your thoughts, nor are your ways My ways', says the Lord. 'For as the heavens are higher than the earth, so are My ways higher than your ways, and My thoughts than your thoughts.'". However, we know from Scripture that His thoughts and His ways are motivated by His great love for mankind. God's greatest desire is to see all humanity *redeemed* and set free from the curse of sin and death. He accomplished that in the person of Jesus, but He is waiting for as many people as possible to get saved before He comes back to get His church. His *delay* in returning is evidence of the reality of His love and presence. 2 Peter 3:9 says, "The Lord is not slack concerning His promise, as some count slackness, but is *longsuffering*, not willing that any should perish but that all should come to repentance." There are still millions of unsaved sinners alive today. Because of His great love for them, God does not want them to eternally perish. The Lord will return at the right time in His perfect will, motivated by love and mercy for the lost.

Jesus suffered on the cross for six hours, from the third hour which is 9 a.m. to the ninth hour which is 3 p.m. It is beyond our comprehension to understand why the God who created the world and all things, including us, would be willing to endure such torture and agony. The Bible says darkness covered the land for three hours, from noon to 3 p.m. During that time the penalty for all the sins of mankind, past, present and future were being poured out on Jesus. Sin is represented by darkness. The Father had to look away during those moments when His perfect Son, the light of the world, was plunged into darkness while all sin was being paid for by His perfect sacrifice. Jesus cried out during that time, "My God, my God, why have you forsaken Me?" in fulfillment of Psalm 22:1. Jesus knew, even to His last breath, that He had to bring to pass every prophetic word ever spoken about Him in the Old Testament. His example of endurance and suffering is what has motivated martyrs through the centuries since. There is no greater symbol of the incredible love of God than the cross.

For centuries God had been patient with His people Israel before He came to earth as Immanuel. Just as He has been patient for over 2000 years since Jesus died on the cross to see salvation brought to bear, so He was also patient with the ups and downs and rebellious nature of His chosen people. He gave them the Law to reveal their sin. He gave them judges. He allowed them to have kings. He sent prophets, many of whom were rejected and persecuted. His *longsuffering* with His people mirrors and foreshadows His *longsuffering* with us. We must always remember those six hours Jesus endured for us when we tend to stray as His sheep. His agony blotted out the sin that tries to entangle us daily. Hebrews 12:2 says, "looking unto Jesus, the author and finisher of our faith, who for the joy that was set before

Him endured the cross, despising the shame, and has sat down at the right hand of the throne of God."

A scripture that brings perspective to the patience of God as compared to the patience of men is 2 Peter 3:8, which says, "But, beloved, do not forget this one thing, that with the Lord one day is as a thousand years, and a thousand years as one day." God sees all of history at a glance. He knows the end from the beginning. That is hard for us to understand, but it is also a wonderful comfort that tells us we can *trust* Him for His perfect timing. He is all-knowing, we are not. He is sovereign and all-powerful, we are not. He is always in control. What a relief that should be to us as we wait patiently for His return.

CHAPTER 12

Overcoming Trials

One of the most asked questions of believers and unbelievers alike is "If you are real, God, why did you let this happen?" Similar questions would be "Why would God allow me to go through this difficulty in life?" and "How could a good God ever permit this tragedy to occur?" Experiencing trials is a commonality among all people whether they believe in God or not. Does God make Himself real through trials? The answer according to Scripture is yes, He does. His motive may be different for believers than for unbelievers. Often unbelievers need to be brought to the end of their rope before calling upon God to help them. Psalm 107:27-30 is a parody of someone who doubts the reality of God, but then comes to a saving knowledge of His grace: "They reel to and fro, and stagger like a drunken man, and are at their wits' end. Then they cry out to the Lord in their trouble, and He brings them out of their distresses. He calms the storm, so that its waves are still. Then they are glad because they are quiet; so He guides them to their desired haven." Often God will allow unbelievers to get to their wits' end to get them to reach out to Him for help. God will use a trial to bring them to salvation.

On the other hand, God will allow trials in the lives of believers to build their faith and bring forth a testimony of His power and presence. James 1:2-3 says, "My brethren, count it all joy when you fall into various trials, knowing that the testing of your faith produces patience." God loves to turn adversities into opportunities. When we learn to wait on God, He can use the trouble we are in as a testimony to others of how He can bring deliverance. When we see how God has moved in our lives, it provides an opportunity to share what He has done with other believers who are going through the same situations. Testimonies of God's power and presence edify the body of Christ. Trials build our faith. Above all, in all trials God gets the glory when we see that He is in control regardless of the circumstances.

When it comes to how God works, hindsight is many times better than foresight. During a storm it can be difficult to see what God is doing. It is in looking back afterwards that we see the hand of God. When the disciples got into the storm on the Sea of Galilee, Jesus was with them sleeping. But He was still in control. We can think that God is asleep or disinterested in what is happening to us. In the end Jesus got up and calmed the wind and the waves. This, along with many other miracles, built the faith of the disciples little by little. God is not hidden, even in the worst storms of life. He is constantly vigilant, moving behind the scenes, allowing this and preventing that, to bring us to the end of the storm trusting Him more.

We currently live in a fallen world full of tragedies and wickedness. Believers in Jesus should view it as one big trial in which God is working behind the scenes to bring about that *certain redemption* in the end. Overcoming trials is a part of the process leading up to that magnificent moment when Jesus returns and makes all things right. In the meantime, God promises in Romans 8:28, "And we know that *all* things work together for good to those who love God, to those who are the called according to His purpose." We will go through many troubles in this life, but once in Christ, He will never leave us nor forsake us, and nothing can separate us from His love. Jesus summed it up best in John 16:33, "These things I have spoken to you, that in Me you may have peace. In the world you will have tribulation; but be of good cheer. I have *overcome* the world."

There is a three-part formula for overcoming trials found in the Psalms. Beginning in verse 7 of Psalm 50 the Lord speaks directly to His people through Asaph the psalmist. In verse 15 the Lord says, "Call upon Me in the day of trouble; I will deliver you, and you shall glorify Me." God's people will always encounter *days of trouble*. The question becomes how His people should react when encountering a day or a season of trouble. The three words "Call upon Me" gives the answer. Step one is to immediately involve the Lord in your situation or circumstance. Don't be paralyzed by fear or doubt. Cry out to Him! This step may have to be repeated many times during the trial. Some troubles last only a day. Others may last for weeks, months, and even years. Calling upon God should be continual to stay connected to the One who is in control of all things. The second step is to wait for and expect the deliverance of God. He may not deliver in the way His people expect or desire. He may require steps of obedience through faith to accomplish deliverance. God may not deliver us "out of the trial" but He will *always* walk with us "through the trial" as we trust and obey Him. The final step in Psalm 50:15 is "you shall glorify Me". Trials, how we deal with them, and above all how we see the hand of God moving throughout them, are always meant to ultimately bring glory to God. It is vital that we always give glory to Him and Him alone when the troubles have finally ceased. Through our acts of faith *during* the trial we can also bring glory to God. He loves to turn troubles into testimonies which can then be used to bring more people to a saving knowledge of His grace. Let Psalm 50:15 be written on the table of our hearts and practiced as the ups and downs of daily life are encountered as followers of Jesus.

CHAPTER 13

Insiders vs. Outsiders

In the Old Testament there was a big difference between those who lived inside the covenant of faith and those who lived outside it. Being born a Jew rather than a Gentile was a big deal. In the temple in Jerusalem the Gentiles could enter only the *outer* court. Notices were placed at the entrances to the *inner* courts that stated that any non-Jew or foreigner who crossed the barrier would be punished by death.[31] In at one sense this barrier was created by a misunderstanding of the heart of God. It was always God's intention to win the Gentiles as well the Jews into the kingdom of God. His plan was to establish His covenant with one people to ultimately win all peoples back unto Himself. But in another sense the Lord made it clear that the Israelites were to separate themselves from the pagan peoples around them to prevent corruption of His chosen people through idol worship. The most important thing to remember is that God's ultimate desire is to turn all *outsiders* into *insiders*. His love is for the whole world and all the people in it.

The God who created the world and everything in it humbled Himself and became a man to facilitate all *outsiders* becoming *insiders*. The death of Jesus on the cross opened the covenant of faith up to all who would believe in His completed work. John 3:16 says, "For God so loved the world that He gave His only begotten Son, that *whoever* believes in Him should not perish but have everlasting life." The *whoever* in that scripture includes all people, Gentile as well as Jew, *outsiders* as well as *insiders*. Jesus even allowed Himself to be regarded as an *outsider* to accomplish that purpose. Hebrews 13:12 says, "Therefore Jesus also, that He might sanctify the people with His own blood, suffered *outside* the gate." Just as Jesus suffered as an *outsider* on the cross, so we as believers may also have to endure persecution and be regarded as *outsiders* even though we have been justified. Hebrews 13:13 says, "Therefore let us go forth to Him, *outside* the camp, bearing His reproach."

Now it becomes our commission as followers of Christ to bring as many *outsiders* as possible to a saving knowledge of His grace before His return. We must have a burden for those who are spiritually speaking still in the *outer* court. They cannot cross the barrier to eternal life with Jesus without accepting Him as their only way to salvation. Rejecting to their last breath the great love of God who sent His Son to die for them leads them to an eternity separated from God forever. It is vital for *insiders* to understand the magnitude of the difference between heaven and hell. That reality should result in praying for, loving on, and witnessing to those still on the *outside*, including those who may think they are on the *inside.* The enemy is relentless, especially in the end times, because he knows his time is short. He brings deception and lies to bear, which, if believed, can separate us from God. Paul warned about it. Peter warned about it. Jesus warned about it. He deceived Eve. He tried to deceive Jesus Himself. He will try to deceive you.

Perhaps the most striking contrast between *insiders* and *outsiders* is presented to us by Jesus in Matthew 7:13-14 where He said, "Enter by the narrow gate; for wide is the gate and broad is the way that leads to destruction, and there are *many* who go in by it. Because narrow is the gate and difficult is the way which leads to life, and there are *few* who find it." Which gate are you going to enter by? Which gate are your loved ones going to enter by? As Jesus said it is a *difficult* way that leads to life. Being a Christian is not easy, especially as the spiritual darkness increases all around us. One of the reasons Jesus said the way is *difficult* is because following Him means *surrendering.* Following Jesus means giving up our self will to follow His will. We are no longer doing the driving. We must allow Jesus to take the wheel. Once we *surrender* control, He promises to never leave us nor forsake us. He promises to be with us in the valleys of life and well as on the mountaintops. He will guide us by His Spirit to our last breath.

The flesh often fights against giving up control. "The spirit indeed is willing, but the flesh is weak." Those are the words of Jesus to His disciples before His arrest in the Garden of Gethsemane when they fell asleep instead of praying. Jesus was saying that their souls desired to do right, but their bodies were weak and susceptible to sin. Even the apostle Paul struggled against the flesh. In 1 Corinthians 9:27 he said, "But I discipline my body and bring it into subjection, lest, when I have preached to others, I myself should become disqualified."

In addition, as believers we must constantly remind ourselves that this world is not our home. We are merely passing through a *corruptible* place on our way to an *incorruptible* place. We should view our lives as a vapor hanging over a lost land waiting to dissipate and reassemble in a glorious land. Hebrews 13:14 says, "For here we have no continuing city, but we seek the one to come." 2 Corinthians 5:4 says, "For we who are in this tent groan, being burdened, not because we want to be unclothed, but further clothed, that mortality may be swallowed up by life." The world has many attractions and temptations. They are nothing compared to what lies ahead for followers of Christ. 2 Corinthians 4:17-18 says, "For our light affliction, which is but for a moment, is working for us a far more exceeding and eternal weight of glory, while we do not look at the things which are seen, but at the things which are not seen. For the things which are seen are temporary, but the things which are not seen are eternal."

Truly surrendered followers of Jesus Christ are all former *outsiders* who have become *insiders*. Through the blood of Christ, we have traded our sin for His righteousness. We have traded our unworthiness for His worthiness. We have traded our horrendous destiny for His glorious destiny. One day we will trade our mortal bodies to become like

His glorious body. By faith in the completed work of Jesus on the cross, we have a legal right to all this trading.

In the world there is an illegal activity known as *insider* trading. Trading stocks on the stock market based on non-public confidential information from sources *inside* the companies being traded is against the law. A person who uses *inside* information can go to jail. Such a person as a public *outsider* has illegally attempted to become an *insider* to gain financial advantage. The good news for us as followers of Jesus Christ is that we have been given *inside* information about the kingdom of God freely through His Word. There are three ways this analogy applies to believers.

First of all, the *insider trading* of our sin for His righteousness is not only scripturally legal but freely given. All that is required is faith in the completed work of Jesus on the cross. We as *outsiders* have been redeemed from the outer court, so to speak, by the blood of the Lamb. Ephesians 2:13 says, "But now in Christ Jesus you who once were far off have been brought near by the blood of Christ."

Secondly, the *insider* information which bought our redemption is not hidden or secret. As a matter of fact, that information is to be proclaimed by us now from the rooftops. Jesus said in Matthew 10:27, "Whatever I tell you in the dark, speak in the light; and what you hear in the ear, preach on the housetops."

Finally, we are to be warned that the enemy will try to give us false *inside* information. He may cloak it in worldliness to make it sound good. He disguises himself as an angel of light. If we become deceived and try to sneak into the inner court in any way other than through *Jesus Christ*, the result will be spiritual death. In John 10:1 Jesus said, "Most assuredly, I say to you, he who does not enter the sheepfold by the door, but climbs up some other way, the same is a thief and a robber."

Jesus is the door. He is the way, the truth and the life. There is no other way to get from the *outer* court to the *inner* court except through Jesus Christ. He is the shepherd who opens the gate to heaven for all His sheep to go in. Sheep are totally dependent on their shepherd for provision and protection. Jesus is the Good Shepherd. He is good to His sheep. Are you a truly surrendered sheep today? If not, just surrender and let Jesus take over your life and guide it today. He loves you and will use you as an *insider* to do wonderful things that will bring many others to salvation. Put all your trust in Jesus and never look back.

EPILOGUE

Many bottles, whether plastic or glass, are often *redeemable*. It is a common thing to see people rummaging through trash cans to pull them out and take them to a place of *redemption*. There are also bottles that have been corrupted to the point where they are beyond *redemption* and are considered *unredeemable*. There is usually no way for a corrupted bottle to be restored so that it can be *redeemed*.

The good news is that in the kingdom of God the seemingly *unredeemable* man or woman can be made new and *redeemed*. God doesn't see any person as trash to be thrown out. He loves every man and woman and desires that they be *redeemed*.

God has made a way for the *unredeemable* to be *redeemed*, and that way is through the completed work of Jesus Christ on the cross. Sinful mankind must simply recognize that sin has made him *unredeemable*. The ultimate price to pay for the corruption of sin is death with no hope of *redemption*. But Jesus paid that price through His own death on the cross. His shed blood erases and pays for all sin. By faith in what Jesus did on our behalf, all mankind which is born *unredeemable* can be *redeemed*. It takes an act of faith in confession and surrender for that to occur. Romans 10:9-10 says, "that if you confess with your mouth the Lord Jesus and believe in your heart that God has raised Him from the dead, you will be saved. For with the heart one believes unto righteousness, and with the mouth confession is made unto salvation."

The road from *unredeemable* to *certain redemption* must pass through the cross. There is no other way. God who created all things came to earth as a man to endure suffering and torture incomprehensible out of His love for us so great. He only asks us to believe what He did and then follow in His footsteps. To reject that way would be totally insensitive and narcissistic, and result in eternal judgment by the same God who made salvation possible.

Psalm 46:7 (NIV) says, "No man can *redeem* the life of another or give to God a *ransom* for them –". Only Jesus is the *Redeemer*. Only Jesus paid the *ransom*. If you are stiff-arming Him today, let go. Let Him take over your life. He loves you beyond measure, and has a wonderful plan for your life.

REFERENCES

1. www.pawnmaster.com/blog
   PawnIndustryStatistics&Figures

2. How Pawnshops Work by Marshall Brain

3. "The Reliability of the Bible: 4 Quick Thoughts"by
   Clayton Kraby from Reasonable Theology

4. "The Reliability of the Bible: 4 Quick Thoughts"by
   Clayton Kraby from Reasonable Theology

5. 30 Bible Verses About Redemption (with commentary)
   from Scripture

6. www.merriam-webster.com/dictionary/chasten

7. Know The Word Study Bible, New King James Version,
   copy 2016 by Thomas Nelson, page 1627

8. Know The Word Study Bible, New King James Version,
   copy 2016 by Thomas Nelson, page 1395

9. www.merriam-webster.com/dictionary/exhorting

10. www.openbible.info/topics/first_coming_of_Jesus_Christ

11. www.davidjeremiah.blog/what_the_Bible_says_about_Christ

12. Know The Word Study Bible, New King James Version, copy 2016 by Thomas Nelson, page 903

13. Know The Word Study Bible, New King James Version, copy 2016 by Thomas Nelson, page 1529

14. Richardson, Don (2005) "Peace Child"by Regal Books ISBN 0830737847 256 pgs.

15. Mondi, John M (2008) "Animal Sacrifice in African traditional religions: a connecting point to Christian witness (case study – the Pokot tribe of Northern Kenya"

16. Lupande, Joseph M., Healey, Joseph G., and Sybertz, Donald F. "The Sukuma Sacrificial Goat and Christianity: A Basis for Inculturation of Africa"

17. Hunter, Margaret "15 Historical Proofs of the Bible"(2013) posted in Amazing Bible Timeline with World History

18. Questions About The Bible: Why Is The Bible Not In Chronological Order (https://bibleint.org/images/pages/PDFs/Chronological-Order.pdf, accessed 2/28/22)

19. Questions About The Bible: Why Is The Bible Not In Chronological Order (https://bibleint.org/images/pages/PDFs/Chronological-Order.pdf, accessed 2/28/22)

20. Bucknell, Paul J. "New Testament Pauline Letters Chronological Order" published in Biblical Foundations For Freedom.

21. Whitten, Russ "Have You Wondered: Is The Bible Historically Accurate?" in The Destin Log published 6/15/17

22. Whitten, Russ "Have You Wondered: Is The Bible Historically Accurate?" in The Destin Log published 6/15/17

23. Franz, Gordon "Benedict's Anchor": Was It From The Shipwreck Of The Apostle Paul On Malta? published in Life and Land

24. 49 thoughts on "15 Historical Proofs of the Bible": Fifth Era: Christ Written by the publishers of The Amazing Bible Timeline with World History

25. Whitten, Russ "Have You Wondered: Is The Bible Historically Accurate?" in The Destin Log published 6/15/17

26. "Ancient Jewish Marriage" in My Jewish Learning https://www.myjewishlearning.com/article/ancient-jewish-marriage/

27. 27. "What is the Significance of 'east' in the Scriptures?" https://hermeneutics.stackexchange.com/questions/448/what-is-the-significance-of-east-in-the-scriptures

28. "Land of Nod" in Wikipedia The Free Encyclopedia

29. "Great Texts of the Bible: The Scapegoat" https://biblehub.com/commentaries/hastings/leviticus/16-22.htm#

30. "Ishmael" in Wikipedia The Free Encyclopedia https://en.wikipedia.org/wiki/Ishmael

31. "What was the Court of the Gentiles in the Jewish temple?" GotQuestions.org 6/12/24